PARAPROFESSIONALS IN
EDUCATION TODAY

Training in the Human Services Series
Steven J. Danish, Ph.D. Editor

Guide to Manpower Training
J. Colbert, Ph.D. and M. Hohn, M.Ed.

Helping Skills Leader's Manual
S. J. Danish, Ph.D. and A. L. Hauer, Ph.D.

Helping Skills Workbook and Manual
S. J. Danish, Ph.D. and A. L. Hauer, Ph.D.

College Programs for Paraprofessionals: A Directory of Degree-Granting Programs in the Human Services
A. Gartner, Ph.D.

Paraprofessionals Today Series Vol. 1, Education
A. Gartner, Ph.D.

The Preparation of Human Service Professionals
A. Gartner, Ph.D.

PARAPROFESSIONALS IN EDUCATION TODAY

Edited by
Alan Gartner
Vivian Carter Jackson
and Frank Riessman

HUMAN SCIENCES PRESS
Formerly *BEHAVIORAL PUBLICATIONS INC.*
72 FIFTH AVENUE, NEW YORK, N.Y. 10011

Library of Congress Catalog Number 76-12419

ISBN: 0-87705-258-1

Copyright © 1977 by Human Sciences Press
72 Fifth Avenue, New York, New York 10011

Printed in the United States of America
789 987654321

Library of Congress Cataloging in Publication Data
Main entry under title:

Paraprofessionals in education today.

  Bibliography: p.
  Includes index.
  1. Teachers' assistants. I. Gartner, Alan.
II. Jackson, Vivian Carter. III. Riessman, Frank,
1924-
LB2844.1.A8P37   371.1'412 76-12419

2151169

ACKNOWLEDGEMENTS

We appreciate the authors' willingness to contribute their articles in support of *Social Policy*. We also want to express our thanks to Gina Schachter for her editorial work and to Mel Freeland for "riding herd" on the manuscripts and for typing them.

CONTENTS

INTRODUCTION

Few developments in education or the human services in general have had the staying power of the paraprofessional movement. A decade after the impetus provided by the antipoverty programs of the mid-1960s, ever increasing numbers of paraprofessionals were working in schools and other educational institutions. This collection of essays attempts to illustrate the diversity of their activities.

At least five major factors have been instrumental in the movement's development:

1. Consumers, particularly the poor and minorities, were troubled by the inadequacies of traditional service delivery and by the reluctance of professionals to understand their needs—both physical and psychological.

2. The poor were barred from achieving professional status by traditional methods of obtaining credentials, which required long periods of education prior to job placement.

1

3. Professionals, who at first were reluctant to accept paraprofessionals, soon accepted them gladly as a buffer between themselves and the poor and minorities. The paraprofessional was sometimes called a bridge to the poor. In a sense, the paraprofessional was the lesser of two evils; the other "evil" was the poor or minority consumer who was highly critical of teachers, social workers, and other human service professionals.

4. There was a need for jobs, and the private sector was not providing them. Consequently, the notion that persons who lived in and understood a community could begin working in it with a minimum amount of training was a positive aspect of the paraprofessional movement and was used to generate needed employment.

5. There was a shortage of personnel, particularly in terms of service delivery in poor neighborhoods, that paraprofessionals could alleviate.

The paraprofessional movement has had a highly redistributive aspect because poor people and minorities now have the opportunity to obtain jobs, education, credentials, and service in greater numbers than they had before. To a considerable extent, it is now taken for granted that persons who lack formal preparation and traditional credentials can do significant work in the human services— not merely relieve the professional of the routine, undesirable jobs. This was not always the case, of course; the opposite view prevailed at the start of New Careers and other paraprofessional programs. Paraprofessionals have since taken on—with considerable success—direct-service work in education, health, the social services, family planning, drug programs, urban planning, police work, and corrections.

This book begins with an article by Don Davies describing the Education Professions Development Act, which set the stage for the development of paraprofessional programs. The next three articles describe paraprofessionals at work with the handicapped (Fafard, El-Mohammed, Gartner, and Schachter) and the children of the poor (Drije and Bowman), two special populations who had been ill-served by the field of education. The schools' failure was not restricted to special populations, however. As Cunningham points out, the schools failed many children, even in the basic area of reading. Here, paraprofessionals provided students with individualized attention, itself one of the innovations of the 1960s. But paraprofessionals were not limited to special populations or specific subject areas. Sweet describes a program in the Minneapolis Public Schools, where paraprofessionals were used across the entire spectrum of the schools' concerns. And Delworth and Brown show that paraprofessionals have begun working in colleges in recent years.

Paraprofessionals are attending college themselves. Murphy describes how these students are faring at the City University of New York, and Carter describes the central characteristics of the Career Opportunities Program, which provides for a college program that enables the paraprofessional to earn a bachelor's degree and eligibility for a teaching license while employed full-time.

In the final article, Arthur Pearl, an inaugurator of the New Careers effort, describes in characteristically bold style what the paraprofessional has been and can be. One important achievement of the paraprofessional movement in general and of the New Careers program in particular has been the widespread acceptance of the fact that poor people—many of whom have lived on welfare for years and lack education, training, and credentials—can quickly learn to provide useful service. In the context of the widely accepted "culture of poverty" view of the poor, this new recognition is an important one for it means that society is learning that "indigenous persons" who lack credentials and advanced degrees can provide services to those who need them. This new awareness is the forerunner of an

increase in large-scale public-service employment programs—programs that would provide jobs for millions of
individuals, largely in the human services. The paraprofessional movement has served as a model for a number of
public service employment bills introduced in Congress in
recent years.

Because the private sector is obviously unable to meet
the demand for full employment in society, we must, in the
last analysis, rely on the public sector. The paraprofessional model has played a major role in helping us to
understand that people who were once excluded can perform jobs that are not only meaningful to them but are
valuable to the community and the society. This is an extremely important dimension in changing attitudes about
"make work," that is, work that provides the employee with
a job but contributes nothing useful to society. In addition,
the fact that 500,000 to a million people have obtained jobs
as paraprofessionals is no minor accomplishment; the data
indicating that paraprofessionals have led to improved human services are also significant.

Paraprofessionals have not, however, led to a tremen-
dous increase in productivity or reorganization of services,
nor have they been a powerful force for radical change.
Instead, these former consumers, as they become workers,
reflect the typical worker-consumer dialectic. As consumers, they are concerned about the nature of the services
they receive; as workers they are concerned with typical
issues such as salaries, fringe benefits, education and training, advancement, and so on. This phenomenon is sometimes described as co-optation; that is, the paraprofessionals come to resemble professionals and make
demands that are typical of union members. We believe
that this is far too simplistic an explanation. Schools, agencies, human service practices, and professionals have
changed as a result of paraprofessional involvement. It is
a two-way process. In some ways, paraprofessionals resem-

ble other students in colleges and professionals in agencies, and in some ways they are different, reflecting their community identification and their own life histories. Although their attitudes and consciousness may not be radical, their very presence in agencies and schools affects the atmosphere and practices there.

Although large numbers of paraprofessionals have worked in schools for almost a decade, only within the past few years have a significant number become teachers. By the end of the 1974–75 academic year, the Career Opportunities Program had graduated more than 4,000 persons, the bulk of whom are teaching in public schools. At the New Careers Training Laboratory, a research study is underway to assess these "new professionals," whose background and preparation differ from those of traditional teachers. Preliminary data indicate that their principals generally rank them "as good as" or "better than" other first-year teachers; classroom observations indicate that they are more likely to support and encourage students than are other first-year teachers; and data about their students indicate that the impact of the former paraprofessionals is greater in both the cognitive and affective areas. Many more studies will be needed to test fully the hypothesis that undergirds the New Careers efforts—namely, persons recruited from nontraditional backgrounds and prepared as professionals in nontraditional ways will be a different type of professional.

In addition to testing this hypothesis and providing a basis for expanding public-service employment programs, the paraprofessional movement is related to several current key themes in education and teacher preparation. The way paraprofessionals are educated is an example of field-based teacher preparation. And because the development of paraprofessional roles involves a careful delineation of the work to be done and the skills necessary to do it (using techniques such as task analysis), the paraprofessional effort fits in well with some aspects of the push for teacher education and certification based on competence. Furthermore, because most paraprofessionals are adults, their education is a piece of the broader development of recurrent or lifelong education, which in many instances involves external degree or "university without walls" designs.

With regard to education, we have already noted the relationship between the development of paraprofessional programs and the thrust for individualization. The paraprofessional movement is also part of the effort to bring school and community closer together. Because paraprofessionals often have diverse work experience before coming to the school, they can be an important resource for career education.

In summary, the paraprofessional in education is a phenomenon that is far more complex and multifaceted than was envisioned a decade or more ago. We hope that this book will illuminate some aspects of that diversity and, in some small way, encourage the further development of the paraprofessional in education.

Chapter 1

EDUCATION PROFESSIONS DEVELOPMENT ACT: AN INSIDE PERSPECTIVE

Don Davies

The Education Professions Development Act (EPDA) came into being near the end of the Johnson era's bonanza of social programs, when hopes were high that federal education programs could help to redress the inadequacies and injustices of society and its institutions. With the possible exception of a few of its programs, EPDA was scheduled to expire in mid-1976—an entirely different period characterized by economic retrenchment and disillusionment about the potency of education and the possibilities of social reform.

Yet despite its brief and turbulent life, EPDA had six important effects on educational attitudes and practices. It helped to (1) create a school-college-community partnership, (2) link staff development and school change, (3) prepare school personnel for a pluralistic society, (4) bring handicapped children into the mainstream of education, (5) encourage evaluation of educational personnel on the basis of performance, and (6) bring more diverse people into education and create new career patterns. The first five effects will be described briefly. The sixth, which is an important aspect of the Career Opportunities Program, will be examined in more detail.

Effects of EPDA

A School-College-Community Partnership

The idea that schools, colleges, and communities should work closely together in planning, carrying out, and evaluating programs for personnel development was viewed by many as a radical and controversial departure from conventional practice. Preparation of teachers has been the traditional preserve of colleges and universities, which made contractual arrangements with school districts for student teaching and observation. These institutions dealt from a position of great strength because of tight and interlocked certification and accreditation regulations and teacher shortages. Almost everybody was perpetually dissatisfied with the results of the system, but especially students, teachers, and school systems. Despite continuous and sometimes harsh criticism, the colleges and universities were, by and large, unresponsive to pleas for major changes.

Salary scales and certification requirements based on courses and credits gave colleges control over the continuing education of in-service teachers as well. Teachers and administrators were generally unhappy about the courses offered, but few districts were willing to devote more than a meager portion of their resources to district-sponsored staff development efforts. Neither the colleges nor the school systems paid much attention to the opinions, concerns, and ideas of the consumers of school services: students, parents, and other citizens of the community.

Conditions went from bad to worse, particularly in urban areas, as it became obvious that the system was incapable of responding adequately to the needs of its markedly changing population of poor, minority, non-English-speaking, or migrant children i.e., children who were different.

The general concept of consumer participation in teacher training was translated by the Bureau of Educational Personnel Development, which administered EPDA, in a variety of forms such as guidelines, materials for applicants, and training and orientation for project directors. Training of Teacher Trainers was the first EPDA program to place great stress on the partnership triad. The Teacher Corps, the Career Opportunities Program, and later the Urban/Rural School Development Program stressed the same theme. In the latter program, the emphasis was shifted to giving community residents a dominant voice in a school development council to which the superintendent and board of a participating district agreed to delegate authority for staffing decisions, allocation of project funds, and basic planning and policy-making. The Leadership Training Institutes, established under EPDA authority for each major program, became the major carriers of the participation concept. The panels of participants working in each institute were deliberately and carefully selected to be broadly representative of teachers, school administrators, students, parents, citizens, and administrators and specialists in higher education. The institutes embodied the notion of parity, which was defined by USOE in somewhat bureaucratic style as "mutual collaborative decision making by those who give and those who receive the service."

The most controversial and important part of the Office of Education's strategy to advance the concept of parity was to give grants for personnel development projects directly to school systems, making it possible for them to negotiate from a position of strength with colleges and universities while encouraging them to include the community in the decision-making process. This move was based on the belief that competition for funding with school systems and competition from alternative training institutions such as teacher centers would be a powerful motivation for teacher-preparation institutions to share some of their power with the schools; a condition of near monopoly was not likely to produce substantial change.

The parity idea did not always work well in practice, however. The results were sometimes messy and ambiguous. Some projects bogged down in intergroup struggles; others met the letter of the partnership requirement but subverted its spirit. Although there is no conclusive evidence that the partnership idea produced better training programs and improved education in the schools, there is enough solid or impressionistic evidence to justify the continuation of the parity idea. At the very least, we know that in scores of projects, college personnel talked and listened to teachers, school administrators, and community representatives in a sustained and systematic way, that some revisions in both college and school-district staff development practices occurred (e.g., more practical experience, more credit for on-the-job activities and learning, more courses and experiences dealing with real community problems and concerns), and that specific mechanisms were established to provide decision-making authority to those who had previously little or none: in other words, teachers and parents.

As already suggested, the parity concept in EPDA should be viewed in the broader context of consumer participation in educational decision-making. Consumerism in education was fueled by the Civil Rights Movement and the youth rebellion of the 1960s and is now a growing and constructive reaction to school systems that have become overly centralized, bureaucratic, and professionalized and to the increased power of teachers' organizations, particularly in urban systems. The next five to ten years will be a time of trial and error and conflict concerning decentralization, citizen participation, and community control. It will also be a time in which much can be learned about productive citizen participation; useful alternative models can be tested and adapted; and the impact of parity on teaching, learning, school organization, and community development and attitudes can be carefully assessed. The result may be a more equitable distribution of power in educational decision-making, institutions that are more responsive to their clients, and a demonstration that our society can regain its capacity for popular democracy. Reaching these objectives is far from assured. Vigorous efforts by citizens and their allies within the schools must continue if citizen participation is to move beyond rhetoric into a genuine shift in the ways schools are governed and educational decisions are made. The EPDA experience with the parity concept can make an important contribution to these efforts.

Staff Development and School Change

One goal of the parity concept is to harness training resources to school reform. Few will argue against the general proposition that the key to change in school programs is a change in the attitudes of teachers, counselors, administrators, and others who serve in the schools. If the schools are to change, the individuals who serve in them must develop new attitudes, knowledge, and skills. This was a basic premise of EPDA. There is a corollary, however: changing individuals is necessary but not sufficient for system change. Students of educational change have elaborated on this point (e.g., Sarason, 1971). An additional corollary is that staff development is most effective when a member of a school staff is involved with his colleagues in a significant effort to review some or all aspects of the school program and plan and carry out new and improved programs. These general notions were reflected in many different ways in EPDA programs. Common themes included on-site training, training entire school staffs together, cadre training, teacher improvement through curriculum development, the best teacher trainer is another teacher, and so forth.

The Urban/Rural School Development Program was the most significant EPDA effort to broaden the concept of training to include the concept of staff development as a necessary component of comprehensive school reform. This same idea was of central importance in the Educational Renewal Plan proposed by the Office of Education in 1971. But the renewal plan went further because it proposed consolidating a variety of project grant programs to provide participating schools and communities with broad authority to assess local needs, support staff development, test and develop new approaches to curriculum and instruction, and change school practices and school organization. The fact that it was a plan for combining funds from different, separate legislative authorities—without any new authorizing legislation—eventually led to congressional action in the summer of 1972 to kill the renewal plan. The central issue between Congress and the Department of Health, Education, and Welfare (HEW) was not the merits of the proposed comprehensive school reform plan but whether HEW had the authority to proceed without legislation.

Included in the proposal for renewal was a plan for funding educational renewal sites (clusters of schools serving large numbers of low-income students) including Teacher Centers. These Teacher Centers, based in part on the successful British experience, were to be important mechanisms for staff development, to be closely linked to planning and change activities in the participating schools, and to provide school staffs with easy access to new ideas, materials, and instructional programs. Four Teacher Center programs were funded by the Office of Education, and others were developed with the support of state and local governments and foundations.

Despite the demise of the Educational Renewal Plan as a program of the Office of Education, there is considerable activity across the country that demonstrates the importance of linking staff development and school change. Although the titles, jargon, and sources of funding will change, the concept is likely to continue to exert a strong influence on both schools and colleges as they seek ways to improve the education of teachers and the effectiveness of schools.

Better Preparation for a Pluralistic Society

The single most significant decision made by the Bureau of Educational Personnel Development about the administration of EPDA was to concentrate about 75 per cent of the available funds on projects directly related to the improvement and equalization of educational opportunities for poor children. This decision did not mean simply assisting compensatory education efforts and helping schools to intensify or improve conventional programs and services. It involved a commitment to change the climate and nature of education for poor children. As such, it included testing, demonstration, and propagation of ways for schools to become multicultural in spirit and content.

The case for bilingualism and cultural pluralism in the schools has its roots in basic knowledge about personal and social development. Positive self-identification and a feeling of self-worth are necessary to motivate children to achieve in school, in work, and in life. Understanding, acceptance, and pride in one's traditions and culture or subculture are important for healthy personality development and for relating positively to individuals and groups that are different.

The schools have traditionally been an important instrument for the Americanization and assimilation of immigrants of all kinds. They can also become an important instrument for building a pluralistic society that recognizes and honors individual and group differences while minimizing racism and intergroup conflict. Therefore, the educational objectives of bilingualism and multiculturalism are as important for the white middle class as they are for ethnic and racial minority groups. As Rivlin and Fraser put it, the need is "to make the cultural diversity that characterizes American society a major asset instead of . . . a problem or . . . a threat [1973, p. 1]."

EPDA efforts toward this end confronted strong barriers of tradition: i.e., the assimilation function of the schools and the overwhelming domination of school curricula by white-Anglo-Saxon-Protestant values, culture, and history. School administrations and faculties were dominated by white middle-class Americans, and teacher-training institutions did little to provide teachers with the knowledge, skills, and attitudes they would need to help shape multicultural schools.

The Training of Teacher Trainers program and other EPDA programs such as the Career Opportunities Program, Bilingual Teacher Training, Urban/Rural School Development, Pupil Personnel Services, and Educational Leadership all made specific contributions to the effort to establish multicultural schools, with the Leadership Training Institutes again serving as vital carriers of the idea through conferences, technical assistance, and reports.

A highly visible and effective effort toward this end was the Conference on Teacher Education and Cultural Pluralism, held in Chicago in May 1971 (Rivlin & Fraser, 1973). This conference resulted in more than 30 recommendations for action to make cultural pluralism a central factor in American education. The Leadership Training Institutes encouraged widespread discussion and follow-up activities in schools, colleges, communities, state educational agencies, and the Office of Education.

Some progress toward accepting cultural pluralism as an objective of the educational system has already been made. EPDA, along with the development of ethnic studies and bilingual education programs, has at least succeeded in bringing the subject before educators and the public. But most of the work remains to be done.

Inclusion of Handicapped Children in the Educational Mainstream

Since the end of World War II, there has been a dramatic increase in the amount of attention paid to the special needs of handicapped children. In the 1950s, concerned parents of mentally retarded and other handicapped children organized a grass-roots citizens' movement that resulted in state legislation and increased state funding and brought about action in local communities. It also led in the 1960s to a substantial new federal program to support research, manpower training, and services for handicapped young people. Although the needs of the handicapped are far from being met, considerable progress has been made.

At the time EPDA entered the scene, approximately 50 per cent of the school children with mental, physical, and emotional handicaps were receiving special services. The remainder were in regular classrooms. At about this time, there was a growing recognition that many, perhaps most handicapped children could be served well in regular classrooms for at least part of each day—if teachers were sensitive and skillful enough to recognize the special needs of these children and to individualize their teaching accordingly and if special services and resources were available in the classroom.

Originally, EPDA did not require the setting aside of funds for personnel to serve the handicapped. But shortly after it was passed, the Bureau of Educational Personnel Development and the Bureau for the Education of the Handicapped agreed to allocate 15 per cent of the EPDA funds for projects to assist personnel serving handicapped children. The two bureaus also agreed that the EPDA contribution would be used to support programs which would make it possible for educational personnel to serve handicapped children adequately in regular classrooms. This agreement was sensible both politically and substantively. The results have been positive and have added substantially to the schools' capacity to serve tens of thousands of handicapped children without isolating them in separate classrooms or schools.

Directed by Maynard Reynolds of the University of Minnesota, the Leadership Training Institute for EPDA's Special Education Program provided technical assistance to every funded project, sponsored training conferences for project staffs and conferences to spread promising ideas and materials, arranged exchange visits across projects, and issued a variety of publications that described and evaluated promising practices.

The importance of the Special Education Program went beyond the needs of handicapped children. It demonstrated the truth of the old and important educational postulate that good teaching is individualized—that 'the teacher must diagnose, understand, and respond to the myriad individual capacities, needs, interests, and concerns found in any group of children. Teachers who can serve the individual needs of handicapped children can serve the individual needs of all children.

Personnel Evaluation Based on Performance

In almost all professions and occupations, state certification or licensing requirements and procedures have been established to control the quality and quantity of new entrants into practice. A long, laborious struggle was required to establish minimum certification standards and mechanisms for institutions that prepared teachers. In teaching, as in most other fields, efforts to raise professional standards and quality of service produced interlocking relationships between preparation programs, state licensing requirements, and mechanisms for the accreditation of preparing institutions. The prevailing notion has been that completion of certain specified courses and credits in an approved institution will guarantee a teacher's competence.

In the late 1960s, the assumption that courses and credits bred competence began to be challenged. The Bureau of Educational Personnel Development joined the challengers and began supporting efforts to place more emphasis on performance or demonstrated competence as the crucial measure of teacher excellence.

There is now a substantial national movement toward performance-based preparation and certification. Several state departments of education as well as universities and the American Association of Colleges for Teacher Education all have significant efforts underway to do the necessary research, development, field testing, and assessment of alternatives to the conventional course-credit-certificate triangle. The Bureau of Educational Personnel Development shares the concern of many who fear that the performance movement may be distorted and develop into an extremely elaborate, mechanistic system based on hundreds of descriptions of specific behaviors to be learned by prospective teachers and to be built into a rigid system of state licensing (without adequate review or participation by citizens). But despite this danger, greater emphasis must be placed on performance as the basis for judging the competence of educational personnel.

More Diverse Personnel and New Career Patterns

Two independent developments exerted a powerful influence on the planning and administration of EPDA: new careers for the poor and new staffing patterns in the schools. Both contributed to the strategies of EPDA planners and found their way into almost all EPDA programs. The results of this influence form an important part of the EPDA legacy.

The New Careers program was first named and comprehensively articulated by Arthur Pearl and Frank Riessman in their landmark book, *New Careers for the Poor.* These authors and others who were thinking, writing, and working along similar lines viewed new and better paying jobs for the poor as essential to break the cycle of poverty. Because they believed that poor people could and should aspire to managerial, paraprofessional, and professional work in the human services, which had traditionally been monopolized by the white middle class, they emphasized the opening up of opportunities in educational, health, and legal services and in agency and organization management. The advocates of the idea saw new careerists meeting the personnel needs of human service agencies and changing the nature and improving the quality and accessibility of these services. Bringing community residents into paraprofessional and professional roles in community service institutions could make these institutions more responsive to the needs of the communities they existed to serve. Accomplishing these objectives would require new training programs and jobs for the poor that would circumvent the impenetrable thicket of academic and credentialing requirements. The Economic Opportunity Act of 1964 (and the Scheuer New Careers Amendment to that act in 1966) was the most important of scores of new federal laws and programs that provided funds for widespread testing and implementation of new careers ideas. As it turned out,

EPDA provided the funds and encouragement for the application of these ideas in the schools.

A parallel movement of school reform, focusing on new staffing patterns, developed in the 1950s and early 1960s—a time when both the number of students and costs were rising rapidly. There was a severe shortage of teachers, and schools were slow to develop new approaches to meet new needs and demands. For example, the schools seemed locked into the rigid, self-contained classroom approach and, at the secondary level, rigid class schedules of 50 to 60 minutes. Ideas emerged for team teaching (two or more professional teachers working with large groups of children) and for the use of auxiliary personnel (teacher aides and other paraprofessionals). In the late 1950s, the teacher-aide experiments funded by the Ford Foundation attracted a substantial amount of attention and strong opposition from educational organizations. In the 1960s, a reform movement developed that encompassed these and several other key objectives such as breaking down instructional and managerial tasks in schools and assigning people with different levels and kinds of training to the diverse tasks and changing the traditional grade structure in elementary schools and the traditional class scheduling in secondary schools. The movement also sought techniques, materials, and organizational schemes to increase the amount of individualized instruction and innovative school architecture to house the new, more flexible organizational and instructional programs. Advocates believed that people in the community could enrich the curricula and compensate for shortages of personnel (e.g., local craftsmen could teach children and parents could serve as volunteer tutors in math).

In contrast with the New Careers focus on urban poverty and minorities, the school reform movement centered on middle-class schools in suburbs and small towns. Its primary motivations included (1) more diverse and individualized curricula, (2) more sensible use of available personnel, and (3) better use of community resources by the schools. The possibilities of testing and implementing these reforms were enhanced by grants from foundations and the Elementary and Secondary Education Act of 1965, especially Title III, which emphasized supplementary services and innovation. EPDA also provided support and encouragement for many ideals of the reform movement.

It did not require much imagination to view the long-range promise of these two related movements in terms of system change. As one of the many reform-minded educators who recognized this potential and was involved in both movements, the author was asked to play an important role in planning and developing the EPDA strategy. During the time that he was executive secretary of the National Commission on Teacher Education and Professional Standards of the National Education Association (1961 to early 1968), the commission sought to become a force within the organized teaching profession to support many of the proposals of the New Careers programs and new staffing patterns. The commission supported the need to open the profession to individuals such as community volunteers, teacher aides, and other auxiliaries and members of minority groups who were becoming more and more dissatisfied with the inadequacies of the public schools their children attended. At the same time, the commission tried to encourage more flexible, field-based training programs for educational personnel.

When the author became head of the Bureau of Educational Personnel Development in early 1968, he brought with him to the Office of Education a commitment to both New Careers and new staffing patterns. The potential of EPDA to support the development and installation of these ideas on a widespread basis was clear. The legislation emphasized serving the needs of those whom Lyndon Johnson called the forgotten Americans. Part A of EPDA talked about recruiting "people from within the community who are otherwise engaged." Part B-2 (the state grant program) emphasized the recruitment and training of teacher aides. Part D called for "programs or projects to train teacher aides and other non-professional educational personnel" and "programs or projects to prepare teachers and other educational personnel to meet the special needs of the socially, culturally, and economically disadvantaged."

Although there was no clear and specific mandate to develop the Career Opportunities (or "differentiated staffing") program, the possibilities were there. Some members of Congress and many educators were extremely critical of the strategies and priorities of the Bureau of Educational Personnel Development, believing that the bureau had misread or ignored the intent of Congress and had run roughshod over the interests of many in the field who continued to support conventional programs such as summer institutes and teacher fellowships in colleges and universities. Some of these complaints and criticisms were justified. The EPDA strategy did place more emphasis than many in Congress or education would have liked on school-college-community partnership, linking staff development and school change, cultural pluralism, including handicapped children in the mainstream of education, competency-based training and certification, and the parallel ideas of new careers for the poor and new staffing patterns.

In developing the EPDA strategy, several ideas from the New Careers and school reform movements seemed especially important if some of the bureau's goals were to be achieved.

1.   The minimum requirements for entering a paraprofessional training program and a first job would have to be reduced or many individuals with great potential would be barred before having a chance to perform and the New Career ideas would therefore be empty rhetoric.

2.   The traditional lockstep of "first we train you, then you work; first you study theory, then you practice" would have to be broken. In efforts to provide new careers for the poor in the schools, it was essential to build on the experiences, interests, and culture of recruits and help them to appreciate the relationship between academic and professional knowledge and skills and high-quality performance on the job. It was also important to the New Careers approach for recruits to receive a full-time and adequate income while working and being trained. Otherwise, an economic requirement would be imposed, making it impossible or difficult for the poor to participate.

3.   Simple concepts of justice meant that the middle-class value of opportunities for promotion and advancement would have to be built into a New Careers program for poor people. Dead-end jobs as teacher aides were not enough. The career-ladder idea provided specific opportunities to move to more demanding and better paying jobs and to pursue training required for higher credentials and academic degrees. Although not all new careerists would want to earn bachelor's or master's degrees and qualify for advanced professional certificates, many would want to and be capable of moving up the ladder and should be encouraged to do so.

4.   An important idea was captured by the somewhat obscure term career lattice. What is now obvious to many persons was only dimly perceived when the EPDA strategy was developed. Preparing individuals for one kind of job (e.g., primary grade teacher) is not enough. Because economic conditions and job markets change, paraprofessionals must learn skills and knowledge that can be applied in a variety of settings. Therefore, it was envisioned that they might begin training and work as classroom aides but move to jobs as library aides and librarians, school-community aides, social workers, assistant kindergarten teachers, and day-care directors.

5. Training and certification requirements would have to be revised so that credits could be given for experience, on-the-job training and learning, and the ability to demonstrate mastery of knowledge or skills without taking a formal course. Giving individuals credit for what they had learned through work and experiences outside the classroom was a central feature of the New Careers idea. Equally important was the concept that performance should be the primary criterion of training and certification programs rather than completion of prescribed courses and the accumulation of academic credits. This concept was important to the realization of the New Careers goals as well as the effort to reform in-service teacher education and teacher certification requirements, including the development of the performance- or competency-based teacher education programs.

6. The New Careers approach made it possible to increase the number of minority and other poor on the staffs of schools and other human service agencies. People from the community would be more knowledgeable about and sensitive to the needs and aspirations of the community being served. New careerists have a strong impact on the nature and quality of the institution's program. These benefits of the New Careers approach were particularly relevant in urban school systems, most of which had a low percentage of minority teachers, administrators, and other staff and were providing grossly inadequate education for minority children.

7. The idea of differentiated staffing—an alternative to the conventional, rigid, self-contained classroom approach to schooling—indicated a recognition of the varying talents and interests of a school staff and the varying and diverse needs and interests of the children served. Differentiated staffing approaches required new kinds of paraprofessional and professional jobs within a school: for example, master teachers (supervisors of teams of profes-

sionals and paraprofessionals), teacher assistants and aides, library and media aides, school managers (who are analogous to hospital administrators), and laboratory assistants. This concept also required different points of entry, different types and levels of preparation and licensing, different pay schedules, more flexible ways of organizing time and materials, and extensive training and retraining for new roles and relationships among diverse staff.

These seven ideas represented important values underlying the planning and implementation of most EPDA programs. The Career Opportunities Program was the largest attempt in the field of education to apply the New Careers idea. The much smaller, differentiated staffing program was a specific and focused demonstration of several aspects of the school reform movement.

Part B-2 of EPDA, the state-grant program, also turned out to be an important vehicle for implementing some of these ideas. At the outset, many who were involved in planning the strategy of the Bureau of Educational Personnel Development were skeptical about the state-grant program. Those of us who had typical liberal-reformer beliefs about state departments of education tended to view them as barriers to change, captives of the educational establishment, and less capable and forward looking than our own bureaucracy. In many ways, we were wrong. Creative planning and work were done in many states with what came to be known widely in the field as B-2. We failed to anticipate the changes in leadership and capacity that were occurring in many states. This downgrading of the potential importance of Part B-2 led us to pay scant attention to documenting and assessing the program in the states and territories. Hence, few hard evaluative data were gathered and little effort was made to pull together data gathered in the states. But it is clear that as a result of B-2, tens of thousands of paraprofessionals who might have been bypassed if the program had not existed were recruited, trained, and brought into the schools. B-2 funds supported a large number of personnel development programs that emphasized the major ideas discussed here as much as did the programs supported directly by the Bureau of Educational Personnel Development.

CONCLUSION

Although conclusive evidence about the success of EPDA and its programs are not yet available, the continuing importance of the ideas described in this article seems to justify the rejection of assertions that EPDA, like other Johnson-era programs, was a failure. Fuller discussions of EPDA and of programs such as the Career Opportunities Program are needed to round out the picture. However, one additional point should be made.

Federal efforts in education aimed at system reform can never make much difference unless there is strong support in other parts of the system. Legislative language, guidelines, the enthusiasm and commitment of federal officials—all can be subverted and submerged. Political realities and pressures tend to erode strong federal initiatives that are not supported strongly elsewhere in the system. The best example is citizen participation in educational decision-making. Federal requirements for citizen participation are inevitably softened and modified in the complex process of adjusting to the concerns of state agencies, local administrators, teacher organizations, and others who are reluctant to share power with paraprofessionals. The system defeats the innovative or radical idea.

The solution to this problem is not tougher guidelines; more specific legislative language; or larger, more effective staffs in the Office of Education. The answer is to take seriously the idea of bringing more power to the people.

This idea should be translated at the local level into genuinely effective mechanisms through which the consumer (student, parent, community citizen) can serve as monitor, watchdog, and counterforce to the system's inherent tendency to resist change. The initiative to create these mechanisms must come from students, parents, and other citizens —not from educators or government agencies.

Reform-minded teachers, administrators, educators of teachers, and government officials can forge alliances with consumer efforts. These alliances could provide the necessary support, readiness, and muscle for the next federal initiative for reform in education—no matter when or in what garb it appears.

REFERENCES

Pearl, A., & Riessman, F. *New careers for the poor*. New York: Free Press, 1965.

Rivlin, H. N., & Fraser, D. M. "Education and teacher education for cultural pluralism." In M. D. Stent, W. R. Hazard, & H. N. Rivlin, *Cultural pluralism in education: A mandate for change*. New York: Appleton-Century-Crofts, 1973.

Sarason, S. *The culture of the school and the problem of change*. Boston: Allyn & Bacon, 1971.

Chapter 2

PARAPROFESSIONALS IN EDUCATION FOR HANDICAPPED CHILDREN

Mary-Beth Fafard, Musette El-Mohammed, Alan Gartner, and Gina Schachter

During the 1960s a broad range of groups asserted, and to a considerable extent achieved, the right to have their voices heard, especially about issues affecting them, and to receive their full entitlement to services (see Gartner & Riessman, 1974).[1] First blacks, then students, and later women challenged the monopoly that made the important decisions concerning their lives and even defined their problems. At the same time, other groups, especially those composed of persons in client relationships (e.g., patients, welfare recipients, prisoners, and the like) asserted their right to participate in decisions that affected them; their right to information, fair treatment, and due process; and their right to decent care and personal autonomy. In summary, groups that had heretofore been excluded, had not been taken seriously, and whose entitlements had been sharply delimited by others who "knew best" have said "Enough!"

During the 1960s and the first half of the 1970s, the human services were characterized by an increase in the number of employees and clients and in the size of budgets —not to mention an increase in attention from the media. Thus it is not surprising that dissatisfied groups have focused primarily on the human services. Nor is it surprising that the primary arena for their challenges has been education, the largest of the human services.

Of special interest is the assertion of the rights of the handicapped—their right to be treated as competent human beings with potential, their right to inclusion and fair treatment. The critical role in this assertion, as in developments in other fields, has been played largely by lay persons such as parents, judges, and legislators. In 1971 three landmark decisions established the right of all mentally retarded children to an education (*Pennsylvania Association for Retarded Children* v. *Commonwealth of Pennsylvania*), the right to an education for all children previously excluded from school (*Mills* v. *Board of Education of the District of Columbia*), and the right of institutionalized persons to treatment (*Wyatt* v. *Stickney*). (See also, *Mental Retardation and the Law,*[2] a new journal that catalogs legal activities involving the right to and quality of services.) In addition, state legislatures have passed laws requiring the provision of educational services to handicapped children, and the opinions of state attorneys general have reflected increasing concern with this issue. The Education of All Handicapped Children Act of 1975 gives expression of and impetus to the "free and appropriate education of all handicapped children."

These efforts, combined with those of the Bureau of Education for the Handicapped and parent and professional groups, have resulted in a sharp increase in the number and range of handicapped children served by the schools. Further expansion of educational programs for the handicapped will result from efforts to include a broader range of handicapped children in the regular educational system (a process called "mainstreaming") and the growing emphasis on programs that are responsive to individual children.

All these activities have direct and immediate consequences for the recruitment, preparation, and use of personnel. Clearly, more personnel will be needed, but also at issue are questions about which personnel will do what and how they should be prepared.

Gartner (1971) found that widespread use of paraprofessionals in the regular educational system not only enables teachers to give students more individual attention but to devote more time to preparing lessons. The obvious outcome was improved instruction. Moreover, studies conducted in Minnesota, Kentucky, California, and Georgia (Gartner, 1974) revealed that when paraprofessionals were used in the classroom the children's reading skills, verbalization, and interactions with one another improved. A survey conducted by the New Careers Training Laboratory (NCTL) (1974a) at Queens College in New York City disclosed that approximately 1,000 American colleges offer degree programs for paraprofessionals in general education.

Although little systematic research has been done on the use of paraprofessionals in educational programs for the handicapped, the literature reveals that there is an increasing need for paraprofessionals in this area, that greater attention must be devoted to their training, and that if specially trained, they can enhance educational programs for handicapped children (Blessing & Cook, 1970; Cortazzo et al., 1971; Cowen et al., 1971; Cruickshank & Haring, 1957; Guess et al., 1971; Olshin, 1971; Terrell et al., 1972).

After examining this evidence, the NCTL staff undertook a comprehensive examination of the present and projected use and current methods of preparing para-

professionals in the field of special education for the handicapped.[1] The purpose of the study was to obtain data that
would enable the staff to develop training models and career ladders for paraprofessionals in this field. The necessary data were obtained by sending questionnaires to state
directors of special education, privately funded organizations whose main interest is the handicapped, and 600
schools listed in the *Directory for Exceptional Children*. To
supplement this information, on-site interviews and observations were conducted in seven states in school systems
that employed paraprofessionals in educational programs
for the handicapped. Paraprofessionals were observed in
team situations with special education teachers and were
interviewed along with the teachers and administrative personnel. The sample was not intended to represent the total
population of paraprofessionals working in the field but to
provide insight into issues of training and utilization that
would have to be considered before training models could
be designed or implemented.

SURVEYS

State Directors of Special Education

State directors of special education provided the following
information: (1) the number of states and territories (total
= 56) that employed paraprofessionals in educational programs for the handicapped as well as the number of paraprofessionals employed, (2) the number of states and
territories that certified paraprofessionals in special education, (3) the number that reimbursed local school systems
for paraprofessionals' salaries, and (4) the projected use of
paraprofessionals in special education. All but two directors returned the questionnaires. Fifty-three of the 54 respondents indicated that paraprofessionals were working

in educational programs for the handicapped. The esti-mated number of paraprofessionals serving in local school districts was 27,000. Table 2.1 shows the estimated number of paraprofessionals employed. Note that only six states (California, Missouri, New York, Pennsylvania, Texas, and Vermont) employed 1,000 or more paraprofessionals in their school systems.

Although the majority of states and territories (42) did not certify paraprofessionals in special education at the time of the survey, certification procedures were already established in American Samoa, Georgia, Hawaii, New Mexico, Ohio, Vermont, West Virginia, Wisconsin, and Washington, D.C. and were pending in Alabama, Massa-chusetts, and Missouri. On the other hand, a majority (34) of state and territorial governments reimbursed local

Table 2.1
Estimated Number of Paraprofessionals Employed by
Public School Systems in the
United States and Its Possessions [a]

Number of paraprofessionals employed	Number of states and territories employing paraprofessionals
0	1
1–50	11
50–100	7
100–200	8
200–300	6
400–600	9
600–1,000	3
1,000–3,000	5
3,000–5,000	0
5,000 or more	1
No estimates available	3[b]
No response	2[c]

[a] Includes the District of Columbia, American Samoa, Guam, Puerto Rico, U.S. Virgin Islands, and the Mariana Islands.
[b] Ohio, New Jersey, and Guam.
[c] Arizona and Tennessee.

school systems for paraprofessionals' salaries. With the exception of Hawaii and Puerto Rico, all respondents anticipated an increase in the number of paraprofessionals serving in programs for handicapped children.

Privately Funded Organizations

The questionnaire sent to 19 privately funded organizations that sponsor special educational programs for handicapped children asked the following questions: (1) What are the functions of paraprofessionals currently working in these programs? (2) How will paraprofessionals be utilized in special education during the next decade? (3) What kind of training should they receive? Among the 11 organizations that responded, eight gave specific answers and three either were nonspecific or suggested another source of information.

With regard to current use of paraprofessionals, the eight organizations which provided specific information said that the paraprofessionals working in their programs filled a wide variety of roles, often specific to a particular disability or to a particular section of the country. Two organizations concerned with the visually handicapped reported that paraprofessionals functioned as teacher's assistants or as houseparents in live-in facilities. (Organizations for the deaf also employed paraprofessionals as houseparents.) The National Association of the Deaf listed six capacities in which paraprofessionals were used: interpreters for deaf people, community social service workers, teacher aides, recreation aides, adult education workers, and instructors of others for work with the deaf. The National Easter Seal Society for Crippled Children and Adults employed paraprofessionals in special education and physical restoration programs. Although it had not collected any statistical data on paraprofessionals, the society believed that special education programs depended on paraprofessional personnel to a significant degree.

The majority of organizations predicted that more and more paraprofessionals would be used in special education. Citing the movement toward "normalization" of the mentally retarded, one organization predicted that use of the community as the treatment milieu would open up positions for paraprofessionals such as recreational instructors, parents of group homes, assistants to occupational therapists, and teacher's aides. Another organization not only predicted an increased use but also outlined four broad categories of teacher's aides: assistant teacher, instructional aide, supervisional aide, and clerical aide. Finally, several organizations noted that increased use of paraprofessionals would depend on changes in state legislation, finances, and the conception of the teacher's function.

None of the respondents was certain whether paraprofessionals should be specialists or generalists. All respondents, however, emphasized the paraprofessional's need for training and favored a two-year training program. Some organizations were aware that some community colleges were currently training paraprofessionals to serve in educational programs for the handicapped and hoped that new training designs would remain flexible and care would be exercised to evaluate and recommend each program according to its merits.

Schools for Exceptional Children

The questionnaire sent to 600 state and private schools listed in the *Directory for Exceptional Children* (1972) as having professional staffs of ten or more was designed to ascertain (1) the number of facilities that employed paraprofessionals and the number of paraprofessionals employed, (2) how long paraprofessionals had been used, (3) the activities in which they were engaged, (4) the source of funding for paraprofessionals' salaries, (5) the need for additional paraprofessionals in special education programs, and (6) how they should be used in these programs.

The 348 facilities that completed and returned questionnaires provided a representative sample of those serving the different handicaps. A total of 320 facilities (92 percent of those responding) used paraprofessionals, 24 did not use them, and 4 did not answer the question. The 320 facilities employed a total of about 4,000 paraprofessionals. Over 50 percent (166) employed more than ten paraprofessionals in their educational programs, and over 80 percent (259) of the facilities had been employing paraprofessionals for more than five years. Table 2.2 indicates the number of paraprofessionals employed by these facilities and the length of time they had been utilized.

Although paraprofessionals were used most extensively in activities with individual children and in outdoor

Table 2.2

	Facilities	
	Number	Percentages
Number of paraprofessionals employed		
1 to 5	83	23.9
6 to 10	64	18.4
11 to 15	34	9.8
16 to 20	53	15.2
20 or more	79	22.7
No response	35	10.0
Number of years paraprofessionals had been employed		
1 or less	7	2.0
2 to 4	50	14.4
5 to 7	80	23.0
8 to 10	62	17.8
10 or more	117	33.6
No response	32	9.2

activities, they were actually involved in a wide range of activities (see Table 2.3).

Table 2.3
Activities of Paraprofessionals in
Public and Private Facilities

Activity	Number of facilities[a]	Percentage
Work with individual children in classroom	273	85
Outdoor activities	224	70
Lunch programs, rest periods, and health needs	188	59
Clerical work	136	42
Operating audiovisual equipment	94	29

[a]Many facilities utilized paraprofessionals in more than one capacity.

Many facilities had multiple sources of funding for paraprofessionals' salaries: 135 received federal funding; 193 received state funding; 106, local funding; and 132, private funding.

Concerning the question of the need for additional paraprofessionals in education for the handicapped, 320 facilities indicated such a need, 8 indicated no further need, and 20 did not answer the question.

With regard to how paraprofessionals should be utilized, an overwhelming number of respondents indicated that paraprofessionals should be an integral part of the special education staff. Many replied that paraprofessionals were essential to the provision of individualized, effective educational programs and could contribute insights into the problems of handicapped children. It was emphasized repeatedly that trained paraprofessionals were capable of handling many classroom activities efficiently and effectively.

SITE VISITS

Paraprofessionals were observed working in educational programs for a broad range of handicaps in seven states (California, Florida, Georgia, Minnesota, New York, Oregon, and Pennsylvania), not only to determine the types of classroom activities in which paraprofessionals were used, but the extent of their involvement.

Table 2.4 provides a breakdown of the classes observed by type of handicap. In addition to the observations in self-contained classrooms, there were three of paraprofessionals working in resource rooms with special education teachers and two of paraprofessionals working with itinerant speech teachers. Among the 67 paraprofessionals observed in these three settings, 64 were women and three were men. Although two school systems reported that they employed handicapped paraprofessionals, none were observed or interviewed during the study.

As shown in Table 2.5, classroom observations revealed that paraprofessionals were involved most extensively in activities which enrich individualized instruction to handicapped children, such as helping individual students or small groups of students with their school work, using

Table 2.4
**Number of Classes for Handicapped Children Observed,
by Type of Handicap**

Type of handicap	Number of classes observed
Auditory	6
Emotional	6
Learning	4
Mental retardation (trainable)	10
Mental retardation (educable)	5
Mutiple	3
Orthopedic	5
Speech	2
Visually	0

Table 2.5
Percentage of Paraprofessionals Observed Working in
Facilities for Handicapped Children
by Type of Activity

Activity	Percentage of Paraprofessionals engaged in each activity[a]
Instruction	
Helping individual child with school work	91
Helping small group of children with school work	82
Assisting teacher with instruction	70
Working in small groups with special materials	70
Reading to or playing games with children	67
Initiating and carrying out lessons in the classroom	55
Physical care	
Supervising lavatory, bus duties, play yard, recess	61
Assisting children with health needs	47
Transporting children from room to room	46
Helping children with grooming or dressing	34
Daily classroom routine	
Preparing and arranging room for teacher and children	56
Supervising class when teacher leaves the room	34
Assisting in bulletin boards materials, art	28
Clerical duties (attendance records, correcting of papers, and so forth)	14

[a]Many paraprofessionals were involved in more than one activity.

special materials in small groups, and assisting teachers with instruction.

Paraprofessionals were also observed helping with the physical care of handicapped children. The majority of these observations were made in classes for the trainable mentally retarded, orthopedically handicapped, and multiply handicapped, where paraprofessionals helped children with tasks such as toileting, grooming, or dressing. In addition, they were observed in daily activities such as preparing the classroom, operating equipment, or aiding the teacher with clerical duties. Table 2.5 shows, however, that with the exception of preparing the room for the teacher and children, paraprofessionals are not used extensively in these activities.

There were four activities in which paraprofessionals rarely participated. Only two paraprofessionals were seen disciplining handicapped children, only three were observed working with handicapped children who had been mainstreamed in a regular classroom,[4] and six were viewed working with parents. Finally, no paraprofessionals were observed working in a Youth Tutoring Youth program.

INTERVIEWS

Administrative Personnel

On-site interviews with administrators, paraprofessionals, and special education teachers were conducted in the schools where paraprofessionals were observed. The following information was sought from administrative personnel: (1) how long had paraprofessionals been employed by the school, (2) how much were they paid and did they receive a differential for working in a special education program, (3) how were they recruited, (4) how were they evaluated, (5) what personality characteristics were desirable in paraprofessionals, (6) what were the advantages and disadvantages of using them in programs for the handicapped, (7) what kind of training did they receive, if any, and (8) what suggestions did the administrators have for the development of training programs for paraprofessionals.

The 22 administrators who were interviewed said that their schools had been employing paraprofessionals for an average of 6.4 years at salaries of $2.00 to 3.60 an hour and that these employees did not receive a salary differential for working in special education programs. Paraprofessionals were recruited through the personnel office of the central school board, volunteer programs, special newspaper advertisements, and word of mouth. The majority of schools evaluated the work of their paraprofessional staff informally: these employees were observed, received feedback from teachers, and had periodic consultations with supervisors.

There was general agreement among administrators that experience, flexibility, commitment, maturity, and feeling comfortable around children who were different were desirable characteristics for paraprofessionals. Most agreed that the greatest advantage of using paraprofessionals was the increase in individualized instruction that was available to the children. The only difficulties the administrators encountered were financial problems and problems of communication between teachers and paraprofessionals.

Although most school systems provided paraprofessionals with some type of brief in-service training, none offered preservice training. The administrators and special education teachers interviewed thought that preservice training should be provided and suggested course work and practical training in the following areas: (1) orientation to children with different handicaps, (2) behavioral management, (3) human relations, (4) general methodology, (5) human growth and development, (6) specific skills needed to work with specific categories of handicapped children, and (7) on-the-job training.

Paraprofessionals

Forty-seven paraprofessionals were asked how they had become interested in work with handicapped children, how long they had been employed in a special education program, how many years of school they had completed, what training they desired, what they identified as problem areas, and whether their salaries were adequate

The results of these interviews indicated that the paraprofessionals' desire to work with the handicapped derived from a general interest in children or the need for a job. The average number of years they had spent working in special education programs was 2.6. All the paraprofessionals interviewed were high school graduates and some had attended college. Furthermore, they believed that, prior to employment, paraprofessionals should receive training in the techniques of human relations and behavioral management and be provided with information about handicapped children. Although lack of feedback about their work and lack of recognition were cited as major problems, all the interviewees felt that their salaries were inadequate, given the nature of their jobs and the responsibilities involved.

Special Education Teachers

The information sought from special education teachers included the kinds of activities in which they utilized paraprofessionals and the advantages of using them, whether they had been trained to work with paraprofessionals effectively, and how they provided feedback to paraprofessionals concerning their performance in the classroom.

The majority of the 22 special education teachers interviewed used paraprofessionals in instructional activities and believed that paraprofessionals could be used to greatest advantage to increase the amount of individualized instruction students received. Only one teacher had been trained to work effectively with paraprofessionals. The majority provided informal feedback to paraprofessionals about their performance in the classroom.

CONCLUSION

The results of our study indicate that the use of paraprofessionals in educational programs for handicapped children is wide, if thinly spread and that there are no significant impediments to using them even more intensively. Where they are used, they are well received.

To date there has been little in the way of systematic utilization of paraprofessionals, carefully established job descriptions, or organized training programs on a pre- or in-service basis. Although funding is a key issue, there is widespread recognition of the need to expand the use of paraprofessionals and provide them with relevant training. For this expansion and training to take place in the most sensible manner, those in positions of leadership in federal and state institutions, professional organizations, and higher education must give systematic and concerted attention to using paraprofessionals more effectively in educational programs for handicapped children.

NOTES

1. Gartner and Riessman (1974) discuss this development more fully, particularly as it relates to the emerging service society and new leading forces among consumer groups.

2. A new journal, *Mental Retardation and the Law,* catalogs legal activities concerned with the right to service (care, treatment, education) and its quality.

3. This study was made possible by a grant from the Training Division of the Bureau of Education for the Handicapped, Office of Education, U.S. Department of Health, Education, and Welfare. The opinions presented are those of the authors and do not necessarily represent those of the Office of Education. The findings summarized here are presented in greater detail in the *Utilization and Training of Paraprofessionals in Special Education: Present Status and Future Prospects* (NCTL, 1974b), which contains appendixes, descriptions of training models and career ladders, and task analyses for paraprofessionals in special education programs.

4. Although handicapped children were being mainstreamed in many school systems, only one system used paraprofessionals to help with these children. In another connection, NCTL found that para-

professionals employed by the Waterbury, Vermont, public schools who had worked in a special learning disabilities program were transferred into the regular classes into which these students had been mainstreamed.

REFERENCES

Blessing, K., & Cook, J. *Class size and teacher aides as factors in the achievement of the educable mentally retarded.* Washington, D.C.: Government Printing Office, 1970.

Cortazzo, A., Bradtke, L., Kirkpatrick, W., & Roseblatt, K. Innovations to improve care in an institution for mentally retarded. *Children,* 1971, **18**, 149–154.

Cowen, E., Dorr, D., Sandler, I., & McWilliams, S. Utilization of nonprofessional child-aides in a school mental health program. *Journal of School Psychology,* 1971, **9**, 131–136.

Cruickshank, W., & Haring, N. *Assistants for teachers of exceptional children,* Syracuse, N.Y.: Syracuse University Press, 1957.

Directory for exceptional children. (7th ed.) Boston: Porter Sargent, 1972.

Gartner, A. *Paraprofessionals and their performance: A survey of education, health, and social service programs.* New York: Praeger, 1971.

Gartner, A., & Riessman, F. *The service society and the consumer vanguard.* New York: Harper & Row, 1974.

Guess, D., Smith, J., & Ensminger, E. The role of nonprofessional persons in teaching language skills to mentally retarded children: *Exceptional Children,* 1971, **37**, 447–453.

New Careers Training Laboratory. *Directory of colleges offering degree programs for paraprofessionals.* New York: Author, 1974. (a)

New Careers Training Laboratory. *The utilization and training of paraprofessionals in special education: Present status and future prospects.* New York: Author, 1974 (b)

Olshin, G. Model centers for preschool handicapped children, year II. *Exceptional Children,* 1971, **37**, 665–669.

Terrell, D., Spencer, A., McWilliams, S., & Cowen, E. Description and evaluation of group-work training for nonprofessional aides in a school mental health program. *Psychology in the Schools,* 1972, **9**, 70–75.

Chapter 3

PARAPROFESSIONALS IN PRESCHOOL PROGRAMS: PROJECT HEAD START

A. Carla Drije

Paraprofessionals were introduced into preschool class-rooms beginning in 1965—primarily through Project Head Start. Not only do Head Start programs continue to be a principal setting for paraprofessionals working with pre-school children but they have been a model for other pre-school programs involving paraprofessionals: e.g., prekindergarten programs in public schools funded by Ti-tle I of the Elementary and Secondary Education Act or by combined federal, state, and local funds. Moreover, it was largely as a consequence of research on the effects of the Head Start experience on its graduates that the Follow Through program was introduced in the public schools in 1968. Follow Through employed paraprofessionals as part of a strategy to maintain and reinforce the cognitive devel-opment achieved by Head Start graduates. Because of the range and depth of experience represented, it is instructive to focus on paraprofessionals who work under the Head Start umbrella.

After a general description of programs and para-professionals' involvement in them, this article will describe a sample of paraprofessionals employed as teacher and social service aides in five full-year Head Start centers in metropolitan New York between 1969 and 1971. The following topics will be examined: (1) the backgrounds of these paraprofessionals, (2) the different roles that teacher aides and social service aides played and the structural characteristics of the settings in which they worked, (3) the subjective views of the two groups on how their work affected them and their clients, and (4) the attitudes of supervisors about employing paraprofessionals. Finally, the Head Start's learning and teaching processes related to the work of paraprofessionals will be discussed.

PROGRAMS AND PARAPROFESSIONAL INVOLVEMENT

Project Head Start was established as a Community Action Program (CAP) of the War against Poverty. Its mandate of maximum feasible participation called for an approach to the care of preschool children that included health, nutritional, and social service components as well as the traditional educational goals of cognitive and social development.

A major result of this nontraditional approach was that social service personnel were recruited to work not only with children but with their families as well. Parents were provided with opportunities to increase their knowledge of child development and care, participate in the governance of their Head Start center, and develop skills that will be useful in other school and community organizations. In addition, they often had opportunities to advance their education through classes and tutoring and to obtain jobs and job training.

Thus Head Start centers provided unusual opportunities for paraprofessionals in both teaching and social service. The presence of two kinds of paraprofessionals in the same setting testifies to Head Start's concern for the welfare of the child's family and to its recognition of the family's influence on child development.

Funded through the Office of Child Development of the Department of Health, Education, and Welfare, Project Head Start currently includes three programs: (1) the full-year program, which is the largest and will be discussed in greatest detail, (2) the summer program, and (3) an experimental program. Both the full-year and summer programs are offered in a classroom setting on either a full or half-day schedule to children ages three to six. Since 1973 special services for the handicapped have been a fundamental part of these programs; the Head Start goal has been to achieve a 10 percent enrollment of handicapped children in all its centers and classrooms. In contrast with the full-year and summer programs, experimental programs work with children from different age groups and their parents in different settings. For example, Parent and Child Centers provide services for children from birth to age three, Home Start delivers services to parents and children in their own homes, and the Child and Family Resource Program is designed to provide family-oriented comprehensive child development services to children from the prenatal period through age eight.

In fiscal year 1974, the Head Start programs served 379,000 children, primarily from families with incomes below the poverty level. The provision of services to large numbers of children and their parents is made possible because paraprofessionals are employed in a wide range of roles. Moreover, as Head Start has expanded its services, the opportunities for paraprofessionals to work and train in the different areas and to achieve professional status in a variety of specialities have increased. For example, these paraprofessionals now serve as teacher aides, teacher assistants, home visitors (essentially as educators of adults), social service workers, and health program coordinators.

Head Start's mandate to employ the "indigenous" paraprofessional as a teaching or social service aide in its centers is based largely on the belief that this individual is capable of serving as a bridge between clients and professionals: i.e., she can interpret each group to the other since she shares the experiences of both. Because the paraprofessional is a member of Head Start's target population of the below poverty level families, she presumably shares their life-style and perspective. On the other hand, because of her daily contacts with Head Start professionals and her in-service training, she is knowledgeable about the professional's perspective and goals.

Training and educational opportunities are offered to paraprofessionals for two reasons: to provide them with ongoing work responsibilities and subsequent career advancement. With regard to ongoing work responsibilities, there are no work experience or educational requirements for beginning paraprofessionals in Head Start. In-service training takes place both formally and informally in special classes, courses, and workshops and while carrying out daily responsibilities under professional supervision. Indeed, the professionals in each project are responsible for training and gradually increasing the responsibilities of their paraprofessional assistants.

Opportunity for career advancement was mandated by two amendments to the Equal Opportunity Act in 1965 and 1966. These amendments specified the provision of the "opportunity for further occupational training and career advancement" and a contribution to the "occupational development or upward mobility of individual participants."[1] Head Start's career development program enables paraprofessionals to enroll in college courses and degree programs. In the fall of 1973, Joseph E. Montoya, Director of Career Development and Technical Assistance, stated that "by 1968, 7,000 Head Start staff members were enrolled in early childhood education or related academic programs in higher education institutions across the country. These first trainees (many of whom now have degrees) proved the success of the program [p. 2]."

By September 1974, approximately 10,000 Head Start paraprofessionals were enrolled in college-level courses.

Another training program initiated in 1973 offered paraprofessionals a route to accreditation that differed from the traditional college path. This program, called the Child Development Associate (CDA) competency-based training project, seeks to develop professional workers who will assume responsibility for preschool children in center-based programs. According to Montoya, "the key feature of this project is that unlike the traditional approach to professional training in education, the CDA credential will be based on *demonstrated competency* to work effectively with young children rather than solely upon courses taken, academic credits earned, or degrees conferred [1973, p. 1; italics added]."

The CDA program represents a radical change in the training of professional educators. Although the concept of competency, or teacher training based on performance appeared to be well on the way to being incorporated into the traditional college program before the inception of CDA program, Litman (1971) suggested that Head Start's emphasis on the closely related concept of career development brought new pressure on school systems and agencies to establish behavioral criteria for the selection of teachers and other school personnel.

In 1973, 286,900 children were enrolled in 9,600 full-year centers, with a total staff of 35,433 paraprofessionals and approximately 21,500 professionals. The majority of the paraprofessionals were teacher aides and social service aides; others were employed as food preparation aides and office personnel. Although most professionals were teachers, social workers, and directors of centers, a few mental health professionals such as child therapists, psychologists, and psychiatrists were also employed by the centers, usually on a part-time basis.

A full-year Heat Start center consists of one or more classrooms and offers either a full-day program attended by approximately 20 children, or two half-day sessions, with different groups of approximately 15 children attending each. The classroom staff consists of one teacher and one teacher aide. Parents, other community residents, and even Youth Corps and Urban Corps workers supplement the classroom staff.

Unlike the teacher aides, the social service aides have a choice of several jobs, including parent activities coordinator, health aide, family assistant, and family worker (the titles vary somewhat among programs). A professional social worker either supervises the paraprofessional staff directly on a full- or part-time basis or acts as a consultant to family service workers.

A Survey of Paraprofessionals in Five Full-year Centers

The following data were obtained from a sample of 36 paraprofessionals (18 teacher aides and 18 social service aides) employed in five full-year centers in metropolitan New York.[2]

These subjects will be described in terms of their ethnic background, age, marital and parental status, educational and work experience, place of residence, length of time employed by Head Start and type of employment (i.e., full- or part-time) and previous contacts with Head Start and similar organizations and settings. In addition, we will describe their work responsibilities, the work settings, and the aides' view of their work.

Ethnic Background

The ethnicity of paraprofessionals in any Community Action program should reflect the ethnic composition of the neighborhood in which the center is located. In 1969 and 1970, taking the country as a whole, the different ethnic groups were represented in Head Start in the following proportions: black, 48.2 per cent; white, 24.9 per cent; Mexican-American, 9.4 per cent; Puerto Rican, 5.9 per cent; American Indian, 2.5 per cent; Oriental, 2 per cent; and "other" or "not reported," 8.6 per cent. These percentages have not changed significantly since 1970 (Bates, 1971).

In the summer of 1974, a total of 900 paraprofessionals working in Head Start centers in New York City were ethnically distributed as follows: black, 63 per cent; Spanish-surnamed, 32 per cent; Oriental, 1 per cent; American Indian, less than 1 per cent; and others, including whites, 9 per cent.[3] Obviously, these distributions also reflected the proportions of families with incomes below the poverty level. In part, however, the centers from which the 36 Head Start teachers and social service aides were selected, reflect the country as a whole rather than New York City alone. Therefore, the proportion of whites in the samples, although atypical of Head Start centers in metropolitan New York, was typical of the proportion nationwide. Two of the five centers studied were located in predominantly black neighborhoods, one was situated in a mixed but predominantly Spanish neighborhood, one was in a predominantly white neighborhood, and one was located in a neighborhood of mixed ethnicity and income.

Sex and Age

All except five of the paraprofessionals in the sample were women, and most (approximately 70 per cent) were between the ages of 20 and 34; the majority of them were under 30. The upper range for the remaining 30 per cent was 55.

The fact that 14 per cent of the aides were men—an unusually large percentage, not only for metropolitan New York, but for the nation as a whole—stems from the deliberate policy of two centers to employ men as classroom workers.

Marital and Parental Status

Eighteen subjects were married; nine were separated, widowed, or divorced; and the remainder were unmarried. All but five subjects (three of whom were male), had children. The total number of children was 82; 50 per cent were under 12 years of age and approximately 25 percent were five or younger.

Educational and Employment Background

A substantial majority of the subjects (about 60 per cent) had graduated from high school; about one-third had attended but had not graduated. Six per cent had an eighth-grade education or less. About one-third of the sample had attended college: 22 per cent for two years or less and the remainder for more than two (one had graduated).

The previous work experience of the paraprofessionals (many had held several different jobs; only two had never been employed) was concentrated in three areas: clerical or related work; labor, except farming and mining; and service work, excluding private household. The jobs in these three categories accounted for more than one-half of the total jobs; 28 per cent of the subjects had worked in the first two areas, and one-third had been service workers, excluding private household. (Only one out of 12 responses referred to employment as a domestic worker or cleaning woman.) The following occupational categories accounted for approximately 30 per cent of the total jobs held: operatives and kindred workers; professional, technical, and kindred workers; and paraprofessional workers, except hospital workers.

In summary, only 29 per cent of the subjects' responses referred to previous employment as a laborer or as a domestic or cleaning service worker, contrary to the expectations of the architects of the paraprofessional role. However, approximately 17 per cent of the subjects' responses referred to previous work experience as a clerical or kindred worker, and, as mentioned earlier, slightly less than one out of three previous jobs involved skilled, professional, or paraprofessional work. Indeed, 38 per cent of the responses concerned service work of all kinds and employment as a laborer. In other words, the work experience of the majority of Head Start paraprofessionals did not fall into the occupational categories that had been anticipated. Apparently, for most Head Start subjects, assuming a paraprofessional role—new in the repertoire of occupations— represented the next step up in the occupational heirarchy rather than a leap from an unskilled to a semiprofessional job.

Place of Residence

The 36 aides in the study constituted an indigenous, largely full-time work force, showing a stability of Head Start employment over time. Thirty-one aides lived within 15 blocks of the center where they worked; many lived within five blocks. Almost 75 percent worked full-time; the remainder worked every day on a part-time basis.

Experience in Head Start

Nineteen of the subjects had been employed by Head Start for at least one year (16 had been employed for two to five years). Among the remaining 17 aides, approximately half had worked for Head Start for less than six months and the other half had been employed between six and 12 months.

Eighteen subjects, all of them women, had held previous jobs as Head Start teacher aides (7) or social service aides (11). Ten additional subjects had obtained their experience as classroom volunteers or as participants in parent activity programs in Head Start centers—often those in which they were subsequently employed. Usually their children had been or were still enrolled in the centers where they had served in these capacities. Four teacher aides had been volunteer classroom helpers. Six social service aides had participated in center activities for parents; indeed, three of them had chaired their center's Policy Advisory Committee, the governing body composed of parents.

Seven of the remaining eight subjects with previous experience that was similar to their present work had been salaried. All but one had worked in settings other than Head Start centers. Two teacher aides had been employed in the same position in a nursery school, while one had been an elementary school and kindergarten teacher. Among the five social service aides in this group, four had been hired by Head Start to organize activities for adults (usually parents) and one had worked at her center in this capacity before it had become affiliated with Head Start. Three of the four aides who had organized parent activities also had done extensive volunteer work with public school parent organizations or church groups or with other neighborhood poverty programs. The fifth social service aide, the only one whose experience was not derived from paid work, had been an active volunteer in the local PTA.

Finally, although four subjects had previous experience in either Head Start or a similar setting, this experience was not directly related to their current work. These subjects included one teacher aide who had been chairwoman of the Policy Advisory Committee at the Head Start center her child attended, and three social service aides who had been classroom assistants with preschool children.

THE PARAPROFESSIONAL ROLE: WORK RESPONSIBILITIES

The responsibilities of the 36 Head Start teacher aides and social service aides will be described separately and then compared. Job descriptions are based on the subjects' own perceptions of their roles and tasks are classified according to three categories: child focused, parent focused, and supportive. Unlike the first two categories, the supportive category includes responsibilities that entail little direct personal contact with children or parents and are primarily supportive of child- or parent-focused responsibilities.

Teacher Aides

Among the 18 teacher aides, more than half of all tasks named were child focused. A large majority of these aides mentioned responsibilities such as "stimulating and guiding" the children and "custodial child care." The first task included duties such as supervising a specific activity or attempting to interest a child in an activity when he cannot decide what to do. Custodial care might include escorting a child to the bathroom or helping him to dress.

Forty percent of the teacher aides' responses were related to supportive tasks such as "housekeeping," which included maintaining supplies and cleaning and dusting equipment, and "planning the curriculum." Nine aides mentioned the first task and six mentioned the second. Only 7 percent of the teacher aides' responses referred to parent-focused responsibilities such as answering parents' questions about their children and visiting the children's homes.

Social Service Aides

Before describing the social service aides' duties, it should be noted that six of these aides were called family assistants and 12 were called family workers. Although their roles were similar, family assistants assumed more responsibility for organizational work with parents and sometimes supervised the family workers.

Two-thirds of the tasks mentioned by all the social aides involved direct contact with parents and children.

Parent-focused tasks involved services such as helping parents negotiate with housing, legal, or health agencies; visiting the children's homes; and guiding the center's governance activities. Child-focused responsibilities included escorting children to and from the center when the parent was unable to do so; baby-sitting and other child care activities such as helping the teachers during classroom excursions and caring for students or their siblings when a mother is in a meeting or has medical, housing, or court appointments; and facilitating the children's health care by escorting them to clinics and health care centers.

Parent-focused tasks were mentioned approximately 2½ times as often as were child-focused tasks (47 per cent versus 20 per cent). Yet, generally speaking, the social service aides described their role as involving contact with the entire family—the very focus of their job titles.

The fact that one-third of all responses included supportive tasks indicates the diversity of the social service aide's responsibilities. This category includes duties such as substituting for absent staff members, assisting wherever needed, and maintaining a list of community resources that might be useful to families. Clearly, the social service aides viewed their roles as including a wide variety of tasks that involved them not only in diverse aspects of the center's activities but in the local community and the city.

Comparison of Roles

A brief comparison of the role descriptions of the two groups shows that the social service aides' tasks were more evenly distributed among the child-focused, parent-focused, and supportive categories than were those of the teacher aides. For example, the social service aides mentioned tasks that involved direct contact with children 20 per cent of the time, while teacher aides mentioned parent-focused tasks only 7 per cent of the time. This is not surprising, considering the centers' primary focus on preschool children and the specific policies and practices of Project Head Start. For example, the provision of escort services for children to the center or to a clinic or hospital is unusual in nursery-school settings. In addition, Head Start's essential concern with the families of its students is reflected in the provision of baby-sitting services. The primary focus of the teacher aides' responsibilities appears to be the classroom because of all the child care, teaching, and supporting activities taking place there.

STRUCTURAL CHARACTERISTICS OF WORK SETTINGS

As a background for examining the aides' perceptions of their jobs, the following structural characteristics of the setting in which each group worked will be compared: (1) relationship to immediate supervisors, (2) visibility of work, (3) content of work role, (4) effect of work, and (5) opportunities for promotion.

Relationships with professional supervisors. Teacher aides and social service aides differed in two ways in this respect. First, the two groups differed in the extent to which they performed their work in the presence of the supervisor. The teacher aide usually worked side by side with the teacher. Therefore, even if the teacher aide assumed a leadership role, such as introducing a new project or leading an activity, he or she usually did so in the teacher's presence.

The social service aide, on the other hand, carried out many of her responsibilities outside the center and thus her supervisor could not observe her work directly. And even when she performed tasks within the center, she did not necessarily do so in the supervisor's presence. Moreover, because the social service director did not always work full-time at a particular center, the social service aide had fewer opportunities to obtain advice based on her observed performance than did the teacher aide. It should be noted, however, that this difference was inherent in the nature of the two jobs. That is, more social work than teaching tasks are performed independently. Even when a teacher aide worked alone, e.g., with an individual child in the classroom, her work could be observed.

Visibility of work. A far higher proportion of the work done by teacher aides was visible than was that of the social service aide, whose work often took her out of the center for a considerable portion of the day. In addition, even when the social service aide worked at the center (e.g., when counseling individual parents), she often required privacy to do so. On the whole, the social service aide's performance was less visible than that of the teacher aide's because of the former's mobility and enforced privacy.

Content of work role. The content of the work of the two groups of aides differed with respect to its principal focus as well as the routine each involved. As noted earlier, the teacher aides emphasized child-focused tasks, while social service aides emphasized parent-focused tasks. Social service aides, however, included child-focused responsibilities in their role descriptions almost three times as often as the teacher aides named parent-focused tasks. Thus, the responsibilities of social service aides seem more diverse than those of the teacher aides. The social service aides are engaged in aspects of both casework and group work and work with both children and adults. The focus of the teacher aide's work, on the other hand, was more often confined to children.

The second difference in work content between the two groups concerns their work routines. The social service aides' responsibilities were more heterogeneous. For instance, they sometimes handled emergencies that arose in the children's families—e.g., sudden illness, eviction, or housing fires—in addition to their routine responsibilities. Because the teacher aides' responsibilities focused on the children in the center's classroom, their routine was less likely to be interrupted. Even when a child became ill, for example, it was the social service staff's job to take him home or to the hospital.

In addition, the social service aide's work day did not end until all children had left the center. Consequently, she often had to wait with those who were picked up late and sometimes was called on to escort children to their homes. This represented another open-ended responsibility that the teacher aide did not have.

Effect of work. Although a considerable portion of the social service aide's tasks involved direct contact with children, she was primarily responsible for parents: e.g., helping them participate effectively in governance activities and volunteer work at the center, furthering their education, and so forth. Thus her responsibilities were analogous to the teaching staff's responsibilities toward the children. The teaching staff attempted to provide each child with the maximum possible head start toward his future education. But bringing about change in young children is generally less difficult than bringing about change in adults. Therefore, if the aides' success was measured by the extent of desirable change among clients, the social service aide was less likely to see evidence of success in her work.

Opportunities for promotion. Because there were two

types of social service aide—family assistant and family worker—and only one type of teacher aide, the social service aide not only had the opportunity for promotion within her paraprofessional status but, by becoming a family assistant, also had the opportunity to assume some supervisory responsibility for the family worker.

PARAPROFESSIONALS' VIEWS ON THE IMPACT OF THEIR WORK

Paraprofessionals in the Head Start centers studied were asked the following open-ended questions about the subjective meaning of their work: Has your work here affected your life generally in any way? What meaning would you say this job has in your life generally? What part would you say your job plays in your life generally? These questions were part of an interview guide that tapped other aspects of the paraprofessional work experience.

The subjects' positive responses fell into five categories: (1) increased knowledge and skills, (2) personal gratification, (3) altruistic notions of work, (4) self-confidence, and, (5) self-esteem. The overwhelming majority of the subjects' responses fit into these categories. Responses that implied some dissatisfaction were expressed infrequently.

The responses of the teacher aides will be summarized first. A few quotations will be included as illustrations. Then the two groups will be compared in terms of the five categories of positive and negative responses. Details of the content of the responses will be included in this comparison.

Views of Teacher Aides

Personal gratification, increased knowledge and skills, and self-confidence were mentioned with almost equal frequency by 60 to 70 percent of the teacher aides. Only about one-third, however, alluded to self-esteem or altruistic notions of work.

Personal gratification, the category mentioned most frequently, was expressed as gratification with current or anticipated personal well-being or as positive feelings about the children. For example, one-third of the teacher aides (only one was a high-school graduate) had aspirations to continue their education. One said that the work had given her a "direction, a goal. I really feel that I can finish school and go on to teaching. My whole life is centered on that." (As of January 1973, this aide was completing her final year of a B.A. program in education). Another subject expressed her sense of well-being this way: "To me, it's like freedom, getting away from the same routine every day, away from the house. Even though it's responsibility, it's still like freedom to me. Instead of just cleaning, cooking, washing clothes, going to the store, it's something different, coming out and doing some work." Other aides said they felt happier, enjoyed undertaking responsibilities outside their homes, or enjoyed being with the children.

One subject expressed her feelings of increased self-esteem as follows: "It made me respectable!" Her teacher aide position was a job, "that I can really talk about because I can tell you, before it was just doing day's [domestic] work or something like that—and nobody wants to talk about day's work!"

Only four teacher aides made negative or equivocal remarks about their work, and their remarks focused on lack of confidence in and lack of a sense of accomplishment in their work.

Views of Social Service Aides

Between 60 and 70 percent of the social service aides made comments that fit into the categories of knowledge and skills, personal gratification, altruistic notions of work, and self-confidence. Only one-third alluded to the fifth category, self-esteem.

Altruistic notions of work (mentioned by two-thirds of the social service aides) focused on parents, usually in general terms such as "I help them." Sometimes, however, the goals of this help were specified. One aide spoke of how meaningful it was to parents to be listened to "even if you have to stay two hours sitting in one position . . . because this mother is just cleaning up all of her emotions." Another aide described her work as "an important job. The world won't fall down, but it is sort of important [because] these people really hurt." Other aides stressed the need to build a mother's self-confidence. Their goal was to help parents assert their rights and fulfill their responsibilities in their associations with the Head Start center and the public school.

Approximately 60 per cent of the aides indicated that they derived self-confidence from their work. For example, one aide said: "I'm exploring things I *never* did. If they asked me at first if I could do it, I would say no. Now I know I could do it." Another said that her work "took some of the shyness out of me. I can talk to people because I *have* to do it with parents."

Only three aides made negative and equivocal responses, all of which involved lack of self-confidence. The three aides also referred to impediments to accomplishing the goals of their job and attributed them to administrative practices and difficulties in contacting parents.

Differences between the Two Groups

The two groups of aides made remarkably similar positive responses about the effects of their work, with the exception of altruistic notions. Eleven social service aides but only five teacher aides alluded to altruism.

Most of the subjects' responses were related to the first three categories: personal gratification (26 responses), increased knowledge and skills (23 responses), and self-confidence (22 responses). Unlike teacher aides, social service aides from only three centers alluded to self-esteem in their responses.

Personal gratification. Some interesting agreements and contrasts exist between responses within the categories. The first category, "personal gratification," which was mentioned by 13 members of each group, shared several common focuses: subjects felt better and happier since they had been working for Head Start and derived pleasure from working with children or adults. A larger percentage of social service aides mentioned salary, while more teacher aides expressed a desire to continue their education. Finally, only social service aides were satisfied with the following working conditions: the length of the working day (which meshed with their own children's schedules), the nearness to their children when they were enrolled in the center, and their mobility when carrying out various tasks. The comments of the two groups reflected the conditions of their work. For example, the social service aides made home visits, accompanied parents to city agencies, and took children to medical clinics; the teacher aides, on the other hand, were confined to the classroom.

Opportunities for further education were available to both groups of aides, and the salaries of teacher aides and family workers were equal. Although the starting salary for family assistants was slightly higher, the fact that the same proportion of family workers and family assistants referred to salary, suggests that the family assistants did not emphasize this factor. The social service aides may have mentioned salary more often than did the teacher aides because a greater number of the former were supporting themselves and their children.

Increased knowledge and skills. The common emphasis by

all aides on their own children stands out. Nearly half the aides in each group referred to gaining experience related to child rearing and learning about institutions and facilities that affected their children (e.g., schools and medical groups). This common emphasis was perhaps related to Head Start's primary focus on children and the social service staff's contact with them and to the aides' concern for their own families.

In other areas included in this category, however, the two groups differed. Teacher aides alone mentioned self-understanding and knowledge of child development. Social service aides, on the other hand, named knowledge of the Head Start organization and governmental bodies, understanding of other adults, and specific work skills twice as often as did teacher aides. These contrasting emphases largely reflect the different responsibilities of the two groups. For example, social service aides, because their primary focus was adults, had more contact with Head Start's governing apparatus and with community facilities. It is curious, however, that despite their focus on adults, none of them referred to increased self-understanding.

The underlying theme of most of the aides' comments related to this category was increased competence. The areas they mentioned were predictable, considering the goals of Project Head Start: e.g., the growth of paraprofessional staff and parents in, for example, their "parenting" skills and their competence in dealing with their environment. Thus their responses can be viewed as affirming the relevance of Head Start's goals to their lives. Moreover, their feelings of increased competence indicate that some of the program's goals concerning paraprofessionals were attained.

Altruistic notions of work. Although both groups emphasized the benefits of their work for the children and their families, the social service aides stressed the importance of their work somewhat more often than did the teacher aides.

All aides, however, indicated a desire to view their work as important (see O'Toole, 1972).

Looking at the aides' negative and equivocal responses, one notes that only the social service aides emphasized a specific area of their responsibilities: i.e., the participation of parents in center activities. In contrast, teacher aides spoke in more general terms: for example, referring to a day's work, rather than to an activity or part of the day. This may reflect greater responsibility the social service aides had for parents' "performance" than teacher aides had for the children's achievement. Although both teachers and teacher aides had the same amount of direct contact with the children, the children were ultimately the teacher's responsibility. In contrast, the social service aides not only had far more direct contact with parents than did the social workers but were viewed as uniquely qualified to increase parental participation. Consequently, greater pressure was placed on the social service aides to achieve specific results.

In conclusion, the overwhelming majority of the aides' remarks about the impact of their work were positive. And the few aides who made negative or ambiguous comments also made positive ones. In addition, the focus of their responses was remarkably similar—in most cases, the distribution of responses among the five categories was virtually identical for both groups.

ATTITUDES OF PROFESSIONALS TOWARD PARAPROFESSIONALS

The data concerning the professional staff's attitudes toward the employment of paraprofessionals are derived from a study directed by Dr. Claire Jacobson of the Bank Street College of Education in New York between 1969 and 1971 (Jacobson & Drije, 1973). The professional workers whose comments are reported here were colleagues of many of the paraprofessionals who participated in the study just described.

Twelve teachers and five social workers—all of them women—were interviewed. Six of the teachers were white, five were black, and one was Puerto Rican. Three of the five social workers were black and two were white. All but one teacher had a B.A. degree and four social workers held the M.S.W. degree.

The teachers' attitudes are in the study as follows:

> The attitudes of teachers toward the employment of paraprofessionals are uniformly positive and accepting. Aides are indispensable because the size of classrooms is beyond the managing and teaching capacity of one person. . . . The quality of teaching is improved and children benefit in their learning because more activity areas can be opened and more individual attention can be given. Other themes are that children have the opportunity to relate to different styles of teaching and personalities . . . and that paraprofessionals who are of the same ethnic background as children relate to them better than the teachers do. . . .
>
> Some teachers particularly value the special characteristics which paraprofessionals bring to the job: experience in child rearing, which leads to competence in management of children in the classroom, indigeneity in the community, which implies knowledge of the background of children . . . , and personal qualities such as naturalness and spontaneity, which permit good relationships with children. . . . At [one] center, teachers are particularly appreciative of having male aides because they provide a masculine image, particularly to fatherless children.
>
> Teachers at all but one center state that professional standards are not threatened by the employment of paraprofessionals if the teachers themselves maintain high standards . . . and that standards may become even higher if teachers think of themselves as models for paraprofessionals. . . . At [one] center, one teacher thought that training of aides in the area of early childhood education would improve professional standards and another teacher objected to the "ungrammatical" speech of her aide [Jacobson & Drije, 1973, pp. 107–108].

The professional social workers were considerably less enthusiastic about employing paraprofessionals.

> Although professionals are gratified that paraprofessionals relieve them from performing routine (albeit crucial) chores so that they can concentrate on core social work tasks, they are not satisfied with the general performance of paraprofessionals, their work ethic and the generally poor relations between paraprofessionals and themselves. . . . [In one center] where work relations are not conflictful, the social worker holds a skeptical attitude about the value of paraprofesssionals for the Head Start program: she sees the value of paraprofessional employment as accruing only to paraprofessionals themselves—this is the only type of work for which paraprofessionals, who are deficient in education and job skills, are qualified—rather than to the program.
>
> . . . . Social workers may have been understandably anxious and insecure about the role which might be assigned to them in the future and may have perceived paraprofessionals as threatening competitors. Two social workers . . . state that professional standards of social work can be upheld if paraprofessionals are properly supervised and trained by professional social workers and that centers cannot get along without a strong dose of professional expertise at the center level, which a mere consultant would not be able to provide [Jacobson & Drije, 1973, pp. 195–196].

Some social workers expressed feelings of alienation and attributed them to the presence of paraprofessionals. For example, one worker rejected the idea that paraprofessionals served as a bridge between professionals and parents and claimed that they undermined her relationships with parents. Another said that "unfortunately, Head Start has become the paraprofessionals' program where it is the professional who feels out of place and not part of the Head Start enterprise [Jacobson & Drije, 1971, p. 9]."

The differences in the teachers' and social workers' remarks clearly indicate that the teachers had more positive attitudes about the employment of paraprofessionals. The following factors may explain the social workers' dissatisfaction. First, unlike the teachers, who were familiar with the long-standing tradition of using paraprofessionals in preschool settings, the social workers viewed the use of paraprofessionals in social work as a novelty. Second, the paraprofessionals tended to react differently to teachers and social workers. That is, the paraprofessionals' previous experiences with social workers may have predisposed them to view social workers as dispensors of charity and thus as patronizing the clients. Their earlier contacts with teachers, on the other hand, were more likely to involve positive as well as negative aspects. Third, the social workers and aides had different perspectives about how to approach clients. For example, social workers tended to include psychological causation in their analyses and treatment of clients' problem and to be relatively detached and nondirective with them—"though often manipulating the client toward a predetermined course of action [Jacobson & Drije, 1973, p. 216]." The paraprofessionals usually rejected this approach. "[Their style is direct, authoritative in advice-giving, inactive; relationships with clients are characterized by moral judgment and emotional involvement p. 216]."

Jacobson & Drije also speculated that

> Because paraprofessional social work staff are closely identified with the parents they serve and with whom they share common problems, it may be more difficult for them to adopt the professionally-hallowed attitude of detachment toward them and their problems. . . .
>
> [In contrast,] teacher aides, who are expected to be nurturant toward and supportive of children, may regard such qualities as perfectly congruent with their lay perspective. In teaching there is less of a gap between the professionally-approved way of relating to children and the indigenous interpersonal style and mode of self-presentation. Some objectivity, it is true, is required on the part of teacher aides, but, in contrast with social work aides who are closely identified with parents, they are not so closely identified with the

children that they cannot remove themselves psychologically and adopt a more neutral stance wherein they model themselves on teachers in exploring causes of child behavior and handling problems as teachers do [1973, p. 216].

Finally, both teacher aides and social service aides expressed the impact of their work on themselves and their clients in overwhelmingly positive terms. Therefore, the negative attitudes of the professional social work staff toward the employment of social service aides did not negatively affect the aides' perceptions of the effects of their work.

NOTES

1. Economic Opportunity Act, Title IIB, Section 223, and Title IB, Section 124.

2. The data on which this study were based were derived from a larger study titled "Work relations between professionals and paraprofessionals," directed by Dr. Claire Jacobson, Research Division, Bank Street College of Education, 1968–1972.

3. According to George Tiebel, special assistant to the director of New York City Head Start (personal communication, February 10, 1975), more than 63 percent of the total (900) were teaching or social service aides; the remainder worked as food preparation aides, custodians, and secretaries.

REFERENCES

Bates, B. D. *Project Head Start, 1969–1970. A descriptive report of programs and participants.* Washington, D.C.: Research and Evaluation Division, Office of Child Development, U.S. Department of Health, Education & Welfare, July 1972.

Drije, A. C. *The meaning of work: The paraprofessional experience in teaching and social work.* (Doctoral dissertation, New School for Social Research, New York, 1974).

Jacobson, C., & Drije, A. C. Role relations between professionals and paraprofessionals in Head Start. (Paper presented before the National Association for the Education of Young Children, Minneapolis, Minn., November 5, 1971). New York: Bank Street College of Education, 1971.

Jacobson, C., & Drije, A. C. *The organization of work in a preschool setting: Work relations between professionals and paraprofessionals in four Head Start centers.* New York: Bank Street College of Early Childhood Research Center, July 1973.

Litman, F. Supervision and the involvement of paraprofessionals in early childhood education. In R. H. Anderson & H. G. Shane (Eds.), *As the twig is bent: Reading in early childhood education.* Boston: Houghton Mifflin, 1971.

Montoya, J. E. Project Head Start. *Head Start Newsletter,* 1073 7(1), p. 8.

O'Toole, J. *Work in America.* Cambridge, Mass.: MIT Press, 1972.

Chapter 4

THE PARAPROFESSIONAL IN FOLLOW THROUGH: AN EVALUATION

Garda W. Bowman

For the last seven years, the Follow Through Program of the U.S. Office of Education has provided a broad arena for research on and demonstration of the effectiveness of paraprofessionals in education.[1] This opportunity was enhanced by the essential consonance of purpose and emphases in Follow Through and the Career Opportunities Program (COP) and by the close collaboration between the two programs, with Follow Through providing employment opportunities for paraprofessionals and COP providing training, often of the same persons.

The Follow Through Program is designed to assist the overall development of low-income children enrolled in kindergarten through third grade and to amplify the educational gains these children have made in Head Start and similar preschool programs (see Guidelines for Follow Through, 1974). The program is funded by the U.S. Office of Education and comprises 173 projects located throughout the nation (Cherian, 1973).

To provide continuity of experience for children from Head Start and similar preschool programs, the Follow Through Program implemented seven components of the preschool programs in the early elementary grades: (1) innovative instruction, (2) a program to involve parents and the community, including, among other things, participation in the classroom as observers, volunteers, or paid employees (paraprofessionals), (3) a health component, (4) social services, (5) guidance and psychological services, (6) a nutrition component, and (7) a training and career development program. The employment of nonprofessionals and paraprofessionals as part of the parent and community involvement program is amplified in the 1974 guidelines as follows: "Whenever an opening exists in project staff positions for nonprofessionals or paraprofessionals, the grantee shall actively solicit applications from low-income persons and give preference to such persons in hiring. The highest priority should be accorded to low-income persons who are parents of Follow Through children."

Follow Through Models

The framework exists within which a demonstration of creative participation by paraprofessionals in the education of low-income children in the early elementary grades could and in fact did occur. However, policies and practices concerning paraprofessionals were developed by different projects in vastly different ways, depending in part on local attitudes and experiences, but even more on the theoretical position of the sponsor whose model of early childhood education each project implemented. The attitudes of individual teachers about having another adult in the classroom was another variable.

These models were developed according to a policy of planned variation, designed to explore the effects of a number of promising approaches to the education of low-income children in the early elementary grades. Local projects chose from among 22 possible sponsors the educational approach that coincided with their own goals and objectives.

Although each sponsor had different ideas about the roles and responsibilities of paraprofessionals in its models, all sponsors recognized the importance of paraprofessionals and the basic goals of the federal guidelines were observed throughout the national Follow Through Program.

The basic criterion for selecting paraprofessionals is that they have children in the Follow Through Program. Because Follow Through programs are located in low-income areas, most paraprofessionals involved have low incomes. Another important criterion is the ability to work well with children.

Essentially, the paraprofessional roles are instructional and home-school related. However, Stanford Research Institute has trained paraprofessionals to do testing and classroom observation in a national evaluation program, thus adding another dimension to the repertoire of functions that paraprofessionals can perform.

The following list of Follow Through approaches indicates the variety of roles that paraprofessionals play in the program:

Bilingual-bicultural model. The Southwest Education Development Laboratory in Austin, Texas, requires that the paraprofessional be bilingual. They are trained to instruct children in Spanish. The same training techniques are used for paraprofessionals and for teachers. Paraprofessionals are expected to be sensitive to the needs of the linguistically different and culturally different children as well as interested in and capable of interpreting language materials to these children.

New school approach. The University of North Dakota administers a program in which paraprofessionals work in the classroom, accompany teachers on home visits, and participate in discussions with parents when they come to school. These paraprofessionals are treated as colleagues of the teachers rather than as servants or second-class personnel, and they serve as a link between school, home, and community. When working with Zuni Indians, for example, paraprofessionals are encouraged to converse with children in the Zuni language and record their dictated experience stories in that language. They are also encouraged to teach Zuni to the other children and to the teachers.

Behavior analysis approach. In the program administered by the University of Kansas, classroom instruction consists of programmed instruction and team teaching in specific curricular areas. To facilitate this individualized approach, parents are trained as classroom aides. Responsibilities of teaching are divided by subject matter area among the four-member teaching team. A credentialed teacher generally teaches reading, a full-time parent aide teaches mathematics, and two part-time parent aides teach handwriting and spelling (Nero & Associates, p. 697). Parents are employed in the classroom in a series of positions that provide improved career opportunities. During his first year, the parent works for six to eight weeks in the classroom as a trainee. This relatively short work period enables a large number of parents to have direct contact with the program. At the next level, some parents who have been trainees are employed as aides for an entire semester. Finally, some of those who have been semester aides are employed full-time as teacher aides. The result is a new kind of unity between school and community, new opportunities for parents, and a new potential for truly individualized classroom instruction.

Florida Parent Education Program. In the parent education program administered by the University of Florida, parents are hired to spend part of their time in the classroom assisting teachers, and the visiting families, building parents' home teaching skills. These parent visitors perform the following functions: (1) planning with the teacher for home visits, home teaching tasks, and classroom activities, (2) presenting specific activities once a week in the home for parents to perform with their children, (3) serving as a first line of contact concerning families' needs for medical, dental, psychological, and social services and making referrals through the teacher, and (4) serving as a two-way channel of communication between the school and parents.

These examples indicate not only the variety of functions that paraprofessionals perform but the commonality of respect for and creative use of paraprofessionals. Dr. Gordon J. Klopf, a pioneer in the paraprofessional movement and chairman of Follow Through's National Advisory Committee during the initial planning stage in 1967, was a major force in developing responsible roles for paraprofessionals in Follow Through.

Although it would be advantageous to describe each sponsor's paraprofessional program, space limitation does not permit a full depiction of the scope of paraprofessional participation in Follow Through. Suffice it to say that across all Follow Through models, parents, as paraprofessionals and/or as volunteers, assist teachers in the classroom and serve as a link to the community.

SURVEY OF 14 FOLLOW THROUGH PROJECTS

Bank Street College of Education, the sponsor of 14 Follow Through projects located in the continental United States and Hawaii, was the principal source of information for the following discussion. A questionnaire administered to the directors of the Bank Street Follow Through projects yielded specific information concerning community attitudes about the participation of paraprofessionals in the program. Four aspects of the paraprofessionals' participation were covered: their interaction with children, team-work with teachers, the role of liaison between home and school, and career development.

Interaction with Children in the Classroom

There is always at least one paraprofessional in every class-room in the Bank Street Follow Through project and two if there are more than 25 children. The paraprofessional is treated as a partner in the teaching team, as indicated by the following excerpts from replies by local projects.

> Paraprofessionals in Follow Through perform crucial roles in the classroom. The team teaching in the Follow Through program is the most sophisticated in the school system. The orientation of the assistant teacher is professional in that s/he is performing many instructional tasks and is receiving teacher training.

> The paraprofessionals perform an instructional role in a most sophisticated sense. Not only do they provide support for the teacher in strengthening curriculum, but they also contribute new skills, insights and ideas which enrich the learning environment.

> Teacher assistants plan and work with teachers in individual-izing instruction, helping with small group activities, helping to provide a challenging environment, increasing adult-child interaction and developing intercultural under-standing.

> Paraprofessionals are capable of performing many roles but their main function is to assist the classroom teacher in the daily instruction of children. Often they assume a mother image for the children. Because many of them are mothers, they bring strength to both teacher and child.

These perceptions of the paraprofessional's interac-tion with children were confirmed by the findings of a study of communication patterns of teachers and paraprofession-als in Follow Through the author conducted in 1972 (Bow-man, p. 48). Analysis of communication in all 14 Bank

Street Follow Through programs revealed significant differences in the way teachers and paraprofessionals interact with children (see Table 4-1). The data were analyzed in terms of contrasting pairs of communication patterns: the first pair was considered more related to the goals of the Bank Street Follow Through; the second was considered to be less goal related. For example, stimulation of children's thinking was compared with adult input of facts, as the two contrasting approaches to cognition, the former was more congruent with the project's goals. Supportive communication was contrasted with behavioral

Table 4.1
Differences in Teachers' and Paraprofessionals' Patterns of
Communication with Children in Follow Through Projects
(in percentages)

Type of communication observed	Teachers (No. of observations = 9,141)	Paraprofessionals (No. of observations = 6,758)
Cognition		
Stimulated the children's thinking	41	36
Provided the children with facts	13	13
Difference	28	23
Interactions among children		
Emphasized supportive communications	20	15
Emphasized behavioral control	13	15
Difference	7	0
Praise		
Provided specific praise to individual children	13	16
Provided only vague, generalized praise	1	2
Difference	12	14

control because both affected children's interactions in the classroom, the former in a more positive direction. Specific praise to individual children was compared with vague generalized praise because, although both are reactions to children's efforts, the former is more productive by indicating exactly what was deemed worthy of recognition and thus reinforcing the desirable communication.

The analysis revealed basic similarities between the communication patterns of teachers and paraprofessionals in all 78 classrooms in the Bank Street project. Each classroom was observed for a full day and one hour of observations was recorded. The adults in each classroom were observed for 30 minutes in 15 of which the teacher was coded and in 15 of which the paraprofessional was coded.

The total number of adult communications, measured in terms of the units outlined in Table 4-1, was 15,899, of which 6,758 units were expressed by paraprofessionals. Therefore, it appears that, quantitatively, the paraprofessionals contributed a considerable share of the conversation in language-rich classrooms. The children contributed 13,896 units during the hour of recorded observations.

In qualitative terms, the paraprofessionals also seemed competent. In none of the three pairs of communication patterns did the less goal-related pattern predominate for teachers or paraprofessionals. In terms of support and control, the paraprofessionals had identical scores for both patterns of communication. In this respect there was a statistically significant difference between the teachers and paraprofessionals (at the .001 level of probability) in favor of the teachers. However, in terms of praise, the difference between the teachers' and paraprofessionals' scores (which was not statistically significant) favored the paraprofessionals. Both groups, however, had significantly higher scores on all counts than did their counterparts in the control groups.

Apparently, Follow Through's paraprofessionals accepted and helped to implement the following objectives, as measured by the contrasting patterns of communications: (1) to provide a learning environment in which adults challenge and expand the children's thought processes, (2) to create a supportive climate in which children feel respected as persons and are encouraged to learn, and (3) to give recognition that is related to an individual child's actual accomplishments and therefore reinforces his achievements.

Teamwork

The team approach of Bank Street Follow Through is not only indicated by the results of interaction in the classroom but by the respondents' perceptions of team planning by professional and paraprofessional staffs in all components of the program (instruction, health, nutrition, parent involvement, social services, and psychological services). This fact is attested to in the following excerpts from replies to the questionnaire:

> Joint planning between teachers and teacher assistants occurs daily. Depending on the sophistication of the assistant's teaching skills, the assistant will share partially or equally in short-term and long-term planning for the classroom. Support team meetings occur twice a month for each team and include the staff developer, the parent liaison, and the psychologist. The staff developer, who is responsible for staff development of ten teachers, is a member of the project staff but is trained by Bank Street. In other settings, this individual is called resource teacher, supervisor, or trainer. Support team meetings discuss classroom concerns in relation to the various resource personnel. Ongoing conferencing between the team and staff developer addresses teacher training concerns. Conferencing with the Career Development Coordinator who observes in classrooms on a monthly basis (sometimes more, sometimes less) deals with the training needs of the paraprofessional and the team relationship.

The coordinator is a former paraprofessional who has earned a B.S. degree through the Supplementary Training program.

Paraprofessionals work as colleagues with all other staff members in planning. Teachers and paraprofessionals plan daily; they work as a team with periodic conferences and planning sessions with the resource teachers and the director. They are included in conferences with the sponsor's representatives and attend workshops.

Teacher aides participate actively in team (including staff developer) planning sessions held once a week plus daily short sessions. Parent aides meet weekly with Social Service Coordinator for planning as well as supervision and training. A paraprofessional who works directly with children using his special skill of woodworking meets at intervals with the staff developer, director and teachers to coordinate his curriculum with the classroom scene.

At the end of the day, paraprofessionals sit down with the teacher to plan the work for the next day. Staff developers are a part of this planning especially when there is need to focus in on an individual child's learning style or specific needs.

In a southern city, there was an unusual twist to the team operation. The project required that one member of each team must be black. Both combinations worked.

Liaison between Home and School

The third crucial aspect of paraprofessional participation in Bank Street Follow Through is the role of home-school liaison. Because the national guidelines stress parental involvement and because the parents of Follow Through children are given first priority in becoming paraprofessionals, there is a built-in link between home and school, and the paraprofessional is a central factor in this relationship.

Each project has a parent coordinator and family workers (all of whom are paraprofessionals); many have case aides and health aides as well, and a large number of them are assistants to professional social workers. The fact that the paraprofessionals in this home-school network are appreciated is illustrated in the replies to the questionnaire:

> The perpetual issue of trust between professional (outsider) and the inner-city resident is greatly eased by the paraprofessional[,] who is more or less a member of both camps. Moreover, children and families observe a community person achieving recognition in a professionally oriented role. This affects the paraprofessional's immediate family and provides incentive for the community.

> The neighborhood parent, as a parent activity coordinator, exemplifies the fact that the school values community input and is attempting to develop a more relevant environment for learning. This results in better community involvement in the Follow Through classrooms and increased parent involvement in the Policy Advisory Committee. When, as is preferable, the parent activity coordinator shares language, culture and/or economic background with the population served, his/her contribution can be especially meaningful.

> The health assistant not only provides first aid but also conducts classes in her office on many aspects of health for both students and parents.

The benefits of home visits by health assistants are especially apparent in the rural South, where parents often distrust the advice of professionals. In one southern rural community, the value of home visits was expanded by the development of a Parents' House—an entire house devoted to the activities of and staffed by parents, many of whom are paraprofessionals. In a large metropolitan city, a Parent Room that was organized by an extremely active parent coordinator is in constant use for activities such as study groups, discussions, sewing, hobbies, and committee meetings.

In a city in upstate New York, paraprofessionals conduct workshops for parents and staff, sharing their special skills with colleagues and sometimes with other paraprofessionals in the school district—an interesting example of how paraprofessionals can reach the broader community.

Training and the Career Ladder

Training of paraprofessionals in Bank Street Follow Through has three focuses: inservice training for all paraprofessionals, inservice training at Bank Street College for paraprofessional leaders, and courses at a college or similar institution for paraprofessionals enrolled in the Career Opportunities Program or the Supplementary Training Program.

One important feature of the in-service training, both on-site and at Bank Street College, is the separate and joint training with the professional staff. Separate training provides for the specific needs of paraprofessionals, which are often different from the needs of professionals. Joint training is essential to an effective team operation in the classroom. In a New England city, the Follow Through in-service training is accredited by the local institution of higher education. This in-service plan places great emphasis on regularly scheduled conferencing with members of teaching teams concerning classroom observations by staff developers.

In-service training at Bank Street College provides an opportunity for the exchange of ideas and experiences among Bank Street staff and between projects as well as the opportunity to take advantage of the city's cultural opportunities. The Laboratory School at the College is an invaluable resource in making the model visible, concrete, and attainable.

One New England city has a highly differentiated career ladder with comprehensive job descriptions for each level. This design was developed by the Follow Through Career Development Committee, was approved by the Parents Advisory Council, and was implemented in the Fall of

1972. Supplementary Training is provided by a local college. The appointment of a Career Development Coordinator, who is a graduate of the Supplementary Training Program, was of inestimable value in conceptualizing the design and putting it into operation.

The levels of growth in the career ladder are as follows: Assistant I, Assistant II, Associate I, and Associate II. As paraprofessionals move from one level to the next, they are evaluated on the job with regard to their ability to function as part of a team, to teach, to use materials, keep records, observe children, manage a classroom, communicate and become involved with parents. Although each level has academic requirements, performance on the job is a major factor in promotion.

The comprehensive nature of the evaluation is illustrated by the following criteria for evaluating an Associate I with respect to teamwork.

1. Initiates some planning discussions and participates in long range planning.
2. Is familiar with and able to apply the Bank Street Approach.
3. Participates actively in inservice training. Is able to conduct workshops in interest areas.
4. Continues toward developing good team skills and good team climate.
5. Participates effectively in analysis of Follow Through Program with teacher and support staff.
6. Is realistically self-critical and seeks necessary help in classroom performance.
7. Is learning to understand feelings and perceptions pertaining to team relationships.
8. Is learning to participate in a mutually supportive team effort.

Ten of the 15 full-time teaching assistants and one parent liaison have slots in the local college Supplementary Training Program. This will provide associate's and bachelor's degrees in Early Childhood Education. Five paraprofessionals have received the A.S. and are working on their bachelor of science degrees. Three former Follow Through paraprofessionals received a B.S. through the Supplementary Training Program. One graduate is presently a head teacher in Follow Through; another is the career development coordinator for Follow Through; the third graduate is teaching elsewhere.

Follow Through in this New England city recognizes the A.S. degree by providing a salary jump on the Career Ladder and by acknowledging this accomplishment with the title of associate teacher and an appropriate co-teaching job description.

Brief examples of Career Development in other communities reveal the widespread interest in this aspect of the program. In a rural southern community 22 paraprofessionals are enrolled in a Career Opportunities Program at a local institute; 13 graduated in May 1975. In a city in upstate New York, 25 paraprofessionals are enrolled in the Career Development program at the local college. Three of them have already graduated and 17 have attained an A.A. In a small New England town, eight paraprofessionals have obtained A.A. degrees, and another eight are well on their way to reaching that goal. Some are working for a bachelor's degree; others are taking time out after obtaining an A.A. degree to assess whether additional formal training is necessary to achieve their goals.

There is wide acclaim for the teaching ability of Follow Through paraprofessionals who have graduated and have been certified. But because teaching opportunities are unavailable in some communities, the graduates had to continue in a helping role, rather than assume leadership roles —a disappointment to all concerned.

In most of the projects, paraprofessionals who were enrolled in college programs were perceived as moving up a career ladder rather than a career lattice (which connoted an opportunity to transfer to another field in which their special talents could be used more effectively). However, two of the projects that responded to the questionnaire reported that paraprofessionals had transferred to more appropriate occupations. In a community in the western United States, some paraprofessionals left the program for careers in commerce or industry. One small New England town reported that three of the program's best achievers left the program: one had become an aide to a school nurse, the second was the director of a satellite day care center, and the third tutored a blind child. The six-week orientation program in that community enabled early recognition of individuals who might fit better into another occupation and also assessed the characteristics that would help to match paraprofessionals with teachers.

In a city in upstate New York, the career ladder begins with the high-school equivalency course sponsored by the Parent Advisory Committee. Four teacher aides have graduated from this course. In this community, Follow Through has played an important role in community efforts that led to a study of the feasibility of offering a human services certificate and eventually an associate degree conducted by the local community college.

An interesting feature of Career Development in another city in upstate New York is that Title I has cooperated with Follow Through by offering paraprofessionals a Personal Development Plan to encourage them to qualify for positions in the public schools. It is also noteworthy that life experience, as well as academic accomplishment and on-the-job performance, is a criterion for promotion in some communities.

PROBLEMS AND SOLUTIONS

Thus far this article has presented a generally positive picture of the paraprofessional in Follow Through. However, the program has its problems. The encouraging aspect of the problem area is that no problem is reported without an accompanying report about how the problem was alleviated or solved. A report from one southern rural community claims that all the problems have been solved after "discussing them as a team and seeking possible solutions together."

In a small New England town, the principle problem stems from the fact that many paraprofessionals must stay at home when their young children are ill. In the regular monthly aides' meetings, this problem was discussed and, with the help of the project nurse, improved medical care and excellent day care services, the absenteeism of these women decreased. In the discussions, paraprofessionals admitted that they had perhaps underestimated their importance as part of the teaching team.

In a New England city, three problems were identified: (1) how to differentiate training to meet the needs of paraprofessionals in a professionally oriented training program, (2) how to deal with stresses in the teaching team relationships, and (3) how to alleviate the pressures of working full-time and participating in a college-level program that required students to carry 12 to 15 credits per year. The advocacy and counseling of the Career Development Coordinator has helped to alleviate these problems. Moreover, the continuing dialogue among staff developers, teachers, and teaching assistants is one of the cardinal factors in relieving problems. An established time for conferencing is important to prevent the building up of frustration and tension. The Coordinator of Supplementary Training at the local college helped to deal with the problem of the heavy work load at home and at school.

In a city in upstate New York, the problem of paraprofessionals' lack of self-confidence sometimes surfaces— a problem which is usually dealt with on an individual or team basis, with the staff developer or project supervisor assuming a counseling role. Sometimes the problem of poor self-image of certain paraprofessionals and other problems may be solved through group discussion in the in-service program.

In a large metropolitan area, the Follow Through Program has dealt with this problem by emphasizing the self-development of each individual paraprofessional. In addition to the usual approach of dialogue, cultural trips for the entire family have been organized and Father's Month at Follow Through has helped to develop more understanding and support in their own homes of the adult as a member of the community.

In some communities, low salaries and lack of fringe benefits cause a high rate of turnover among teacher assistants, resulting in lack of continuity and consistency in the learning-teaching process for children as well as frustration for the paraprofessional. In these instances, the dialogue involves representatives of the school district, and the results have been mixed.

In several communities, a persistent problem has been reported, i.e., that the successful paraprofessional sometimes becomes alienated from the community to which s/he is presumed to provide a connecting link. Parents have sometimes expressed their resentment that paraprofessionals are paid for doing what parents do as volunteers. Volunteer assistance in the classroom has fallen off in these communities. This problem is difficult to solve because it involves persons who do not participate in the meetings organized by the school. The solution appears to lie in the attitude and behavior of the paraprofessional, who is counseled to take an active role in the parent group and in community affairs.

A pervasive problem in all communities is how to develop plans for continued employment of paraprofessionals in the school system if federal or state funding diminishes. One large city had dealt triumphantly with that problem where the concept of the parent as a paraprofessional has been acclaimed as one of the major successes of the Follow Through Program and will be incorporated into the various options to be offered to school districts throughout the city.

In a small New England town, the school board appointed a citizens' committee to study Follow Through and make recommendations for its continuation after the anticipated phase out. The report was extremely positive.

In a New England city, the director of education and the assistant superintendent of schools observed the Follow Through classrooms and recommended that the concept of the paraprofessional be expanded within the school system. The school system is currently deciding whether to adopt a system-wide career ladder for all paraprofessionals which parallels the Follow Through Career Ladder. It is also deciding whether to contract with an institution of higher learning to provide training for paraprofessionals.

In one large metropolitan area, a comprehensive Career Lattice is a reality throughout the school system for thousands of paraprofessionals employed by the Board of Education. This development cannot be attributed to Follow Through alone; it reflects acceptance of the Career Development concept even before federal funds were available for this purpose. With the support of the local teachers union and vigorous leadership, the program has flourished, and its purposes and procedures parallel those of Follow Through.

In most Bank Street-sponsored Follow Through projects, the report is that the school system is gradually accepting and incorporating a paraprofessional program that provides for creative participation in the classroom and in home-school relationships as well as a career ladder or lattice. Follow Through is one federally funded program that continues to demonstrate the benefits of this approach.

CONCLUSION

In essence, Follow Through has been a moving force nationwide for implementing a program for paraprofessionals that not only respects the non-certified school employee as a person and as a prime contributor to quality education but also provides him with the opportunity for professional and personal growth. According to those who answered the questionnaire, paraprofessionals have

- helped to deepen staff's understanding of children,
- facilitated the individualizing of curriculum,
- demonstrated the feasibility of continuing education to their peers,
- supported the parents' struggle to improve the quality of life for their families,
- contributed to the human touch that is so essential to good teaching,
- provided immeasurable insights into the cultures, problems, and strengths of each Follow Through community.
- facilitated the breakdown of the traditionally cold and distant school-community relations,
- stimulated parental involvement in the PAC and in the total program,
- increased the school staff's awareness and support of the child's learning opportunities in the environment beyond the classroom, and
- identified with, supported, and taught one another.

One respondent concluded: "They are a strong group. Their motivation to learn is high. Their leadership potential is great."

Finally, those who have worked with paraprofessionals in Follow Through intend to assist them in any way possible in realizing their potential as individuals and on behalf of the children whose learning and development they foster.

NOTES

1. The author is indebted to Elizabeth C. Gilkeson, who was director of Bank Street Follow Through for the first six years of its operation and chief conceptualizer of the program, for her insights and suggestions.

Chapter 5

PARAPROFESSIONALS IN READING PROGRAMS: A SURVEY

Valerie Gilford

In 1973 a high school graduate brought a suit against the San Francisco Unified School District charging that the school system was responsible for his poor reading ability. This case focused national attention on the schools' denial of a basic right—the right to read.

The plaintiff, who could only read at the fifth-grade level, cited three counts of malpractice against the school system. First, the school misled him and his mother about his reading progress. Second, the district had no right to graduate him from high school unless he could read at least at the eighth-grade level. Third, the school, knowing of his problem, placed him in inappropriate courses, assigned him to teachers who were unable to deal with his deficiencies, and failed to offer the kind of courses that might have helped (Sugarman, 1974).

Unfortunately, the plaintiff's plight was not unique. Each year hundreds of thousands of students who are unable to digest, analyze, and use printed information leave school to join the 19 million functionally illiterate adults who cannot comprehend basic forms such as job applications, drivers' manuals, or loan questionnaires.

An effort to confront the reading crisis, better known as the "war on illiteracy", began in the late 1960s as an outgrowth of public opinion. School reading scores and parents' disappointment over their children's inability to read triggered reactions among community groups and society as a whole. Local school boards, parents, and students —especially in the inner cities—organized, openly expressed their discontent with the schools' inability or failure to deliver high-quality education and services, and demanded action. Moreover, courts, legislators, and taxpayers became concerned about the crippling economic and social effects of large numbers of functional illiterates: e.g., longer unemployment and welfare lines and higher rates of crime and taxation. As a result, public school systems were under increasing pressure to assume more responsibility and become accountable for their students' performance.

School systems, supported by federal legislation and state and local governments, began taking steps to increase the reading level of poor and nonreaders. Basically, there were two areas in which development or redevelopment took place. First, money, efforts, and brainpower were poured into the design and development of special programs, reading centers, relevant curricula, new materials, and instructional equipment. Second, this focus on content brought about a shift in the delivery of instruction—from a system geared to large groups of children to one that focused on individuals or small groups of children.

Finally, these developments created the need for additional personnel in classrooms and reading centers to free teachers and instructors from routine nonprofessional duties so they could direct their efforts to the professional task of instruction. Most important, personnel were needed to provide the type of services and support that would improve reading competency. Thus, as the demand and need for better reading programs, instruction, and support services increased, so did the use of paraprofessional personnel.

NEW ROLES FOR PARAPROFESSIONALS IN READING PROGRAMS

In 1967, the National Education Association (NEA) conducted a survey of the extent to which paraprofessionals were used in the nation's schools and found that one out of five public school teachers (19 per cent) was assisted by paraprofessionals, the majority of whom were teacher aides at the elementary school level. Since 1967 the number of paraprofessionals in education has increased significantly. Estimates now range from 500,000 to one million. The majority of those employed in preschools or elementary schools are working with children in reading-related activities.

Of greater significance than the increase in the *number* of paraprofessionals involved in reading is the increase in the degree of their participation. In 1967, 16 per cent of teachers with classroom aides used them in "lay reading" activities, while only 14 percent used them for small-group or individual instruction related to reading and spelling. In comparison, 95 per cent of the teachers used paraprofessionals for clerical, lunchroom, and playground tasks; 56 per cent wanted to perform all duties related to instruction themselves. Shipp summed up the aide's activities as follows:

> She may have played some part in the instructional process, where, under the supervision of the teacher, she read aloud or told stories, assisted children in the school library, helped

individual students do make-up work, or drilled small
groups or individuals while the teacher worked with another
group [NEA, 1967, p. 32].

In other words, most teachers were reluctant to use paraprofessionals except in clerical and housekeeping functions. As a result, the majority of classroom activities
carried out by aides, including those related to reading,
were noninstructional.

Today, in addition to the traditional clerical and
housekeeping functions, paraprofessionals are actively involved in a broader range of reading activities such as planning, instruction, tutoring, assessment, motivation, and
public relations. In contrast to their once marginal status,
they are now integral members of an educational team that
delivers reading instruction and support services. Not only
has the teacher aide's role expanded, it has increased significantly in terms of the variety of educational settings
where those services are used as well as in terms of the
diversity of the individuals who provided those services
(Mauser, 1972). Initially confined to the traditional classroom setting, paraprofessionals working in reading are
now delivering services in community-based programs, af-
ter-school tutorial programs, special education classes, college reading laboratories, literacy programs in prisons, and
so forth. And males as well as females, community residents, parents, college students, and Vietnam veterans are
among the ranks of those who are making significant contributions to the development of better reading skills.

The new and expanded roles for the paraprofessional
in reading can be attributed to the following factors:

1.   A surge of interest in and emphasis on implementing individualized reading instruction and remediation.

2.   The increasing number of bilingual and minority
group children enrolled in the public schools who experience reading difficulties.

3.   The lack of funds to hire additional professional personnel.

4.   The emergence of a service-oriented society in which the wise use of human power in the service areas is increasing.

5.   The expanded opportunities for paraprofessionals to pursue higher education. Several career advancement programs as well as local unions that represent paraprofessionals have introduced the concept of released time for study.

6.   The introduction of new patterns of school organization such as career lattices and differentiated staffing.

7.   The design, development, and use of pre- and in-service training models for both professionals and paraprofessionals in reading.

8.   The demonstrated ability of paraprofessionals to improve children's reading performance. Early studies (Goralski & Karl, 1968; Gartner, 1971) revealed that the presence of paraprofessionals helped to raise the reading readiness scores of kindergarten pupils on the Metropolitan Reading Test.

READING PARAPROFESSIONALS AT WORK

Depending on their work setting, training, education, and geographic location, reading paraprofessionals provide a range of services that help alleviate learning problems associated with reading. The following efforts are representative of the many programs that demonstrate the existence of new roles for paraprofessionals in reading.

Program for Children of Migrant Workers

Children from bilingual, bicultural backgrounds often suffer sever handicaps in school. Reading is no exception.

For instance, the children of migrant farm workers were the target of a program initiated in California in 1971 and funded through the Migrant Amendment of Title I of the Elementary and Secondary Education Act (ESEA) to improve the reading performance of migrant children in the intermediate grades (Veaco, 1973). The program's major intervention strategy was the use of indigenous paraprofessionals as reading tutors in 34 schools located in the San Joaquin Valley.

Eighty fifth and sixth graders who scored two or more months below grade level, as determined by grade equivalency scores on the pretest of the Comprehensive Test of Basic Skills, received tutoring and participated in an evaluation of the program's impact. Thirty-four women and one man functioned as tutors (a title that differentiated them from teacher aides). Most of the tutors spoke Spanish, were high school graduates, and were the parents of children who attended the schools where they were employed. A few tutors had attended local community colleges for one or two years; none were college graduates.

The tutors worked three to seven hours a day instructing individual children or small groups of children. In preparation for this work, tutors received 60 hours of pre- and in-service training from resource teachers in reading and language development, skill-reinforcement techniques, test administration, and word recognition.

Classroom teachers supervised the tutors while the resource teachers recorded the amount of tutorial assistance that each student received. Once a week each tutor submitted to the resource teacher a record of each child's performance.

At the end of the school year the majority of tutored students showed greater reading gains, based on the posttest of the Comprehensive Test of Basic Skills.

Lay Tutors for Students with Reading Deficits

Paraprofessionals were also used as tutors for a demonstration project in Wagner, South Dakota ("Lay Tutor Reading Improvement Program"). During the 1970–71 school year, 21 paraprofessionals worked with 167 elementary school children (including 58 Native Americans) who had severe reading disabilities. The major objective of the program was to demonstrate that lay tutors could be effective in a one-to-one tutorial relationship with children this age.

Program consultants provided tutors with 80 hours of intensive in-service training, which concentrated on methods of delivering instruction, selection and preparation of materials, and procedures for evaluating the project.

During the school year, the tutors delivered 8,620 hours of services. They worked five hours per day and were observed by project consultants and coordinator. Tutors were required to record each child's progress and submit these records to the teachers and parents. In addition to their teaching activities, they participated in parent-teacher conferences.

Evaluations were based primarily on the students' measurable progress throughout the year and consisted of three parts: test results, changes in the tutors' attitudes, and changes in the teachers' attitudes. An attitudinal scale, administered to tutors and teachers at the beginning and end of the project, revealed a significant difference in the scores of tutors and teachers. When the program ended, the tutors had more positive attitudes about the project than did teachers. Table 5.1 shows the mean scores of the two groups on the pre- and postattitudinal scales. Most of the teachers' negative feelings were attributed to their feelings about having their classrooms interrupted by tutoring activities.

Pre- and post-tests of the Durrell Listening Reading

Test and the Iowa Test of Basic Skills were used to determine the students' improvement. On the Durrell post-test, the mean gain in five of the six grades that participated exceeded the average gain expected between the pre- and post-test.

Black Studies Reading Curriculum

According to educators in East St. Louis, Illinois, black children fall behind whites in reading performance because of lack of academic stimulation from parents and teachers (Rist, 1971). As a counterforce, a black studies reading curriculum was implemented in two of the city's seventh grade classes, and black paraprofessionals, all college freshmen and sophomores, provided academic stimulation, motivation, and encouragement to 127 students. Each paraprofessional was assigned to two students, with student and paraprofessional jointly deciding on assignments and grades.

When the two experimental classes were compared nine months later with two control classes in the same schools, using the pre- and post-tests of the Stanford Diagnostic Reading Test, the mean increase in reading level in the experimental group was 3.4 years; whereas the mean increase in the control group was 0.6 years. (Table 5.2)

Table 5.1
**Amount of Improvement in the Attitudes of Tutors
and Teachers During the Program**
(mean scores)

Type of personnel	Number	Beginning of program	End of program	Mean gain
Teachers	24	102.31	103.58	1.37
Tutors	17	123.82	126.41	2.59

Source: "Lay Tutor Reading Improvement Program," p. 40.

Table 5.2
Differences in Improvement in Reading Level Between
the Experimental Control Groups[a]

Area of Improvement	t Value	Significance
Inferential ability	24.7	$P < .001$
Literal understanding	21.9	$P < .001$
Vocabulary	42.2	$P < .001$

[a]This table is based on the results of the pre- and post-tests the Stanford Diagnostic Reading Test.
Source: Rist, 1971, p. 530.

Career Opportunities Program

Another innovative program that uses paraprofessionals in reading and other educational areas is the Career Opportunities Program (COP). Sponsored by the federal Office of Education and funded under the Education Professions Development Act, COP recruits adults from low-income backgrounds to serve in the public schools as teacher aides, assistants, and so forth, and provides them with training, education, and career advancement, terminating in a college degree in education or a related field. The 135 COP programs across the country share the common goal of improving the learning ability of low-income children. The majority of the programs use paraprofessionals in reading programs.

In Jacksonville, Florida, COP uses paraprofessionals to enhance the delivery of reading instruction and improve children's competency in reading (Drije, 1974). During the 1973–74 school year, paraprofessionals were involved in a language arts program called Improved Communication Skills (ICS). Funded through the ESEA, Title I, ICS was established to address the following problem: 50 per cent of the students in grades one through seven who had received reading remediation had failed to improve. Approximately 50 paraprofessionals, including Vietnam-era veterans, were hired as instructional aides for the project, which served approximately 6,500 students. Other personnel included 42 elementary resource teachers, four secondary reading teachers, one reading specialist, two parental involvement personnel, two reading clinicians, four instructional specialists, six reading-speech therapists, and 21 noninstructional aides.

The instructional aides, together with classroom and resource teachers, formed an instructional team that worked with children in grades one through six. Within the team situation, the aides were involved in the planning, delivery, and reinforcement of reading instruction. On the seventh grade level a two-member instructional team consisting of an aide and a communication skills teacher staffed the reading center in each school. Both aide and teacher taught five lessons per day using a systems approach to develop the students' communication skills. The team was also responsible for the center's ongoing evaluation and compilation of progress reports.

A unique factor in the ICS project was its rigorous and intensive in-service training schedule. Resource teachers and instructional aides who worked with elementary school children were trained in separate and joint group sessions. The training was then evaluated, based on the results of pre- and post-tests. In addition, weekly in-service training sessions concerning methods and materials used in the program were held for instructional aides and classroom teachers in each school. Finally, the program consultant for the elementary grades held bimonthly meetings with instructional aides to develop their skills. In-service training for the seventh-grade teaching teams consisted of two afternoon workshops per month, conducted by the consultant. Both teachers and aides were given criterion-reference tests periodically to check the development of their skills.

The broad scope of in-service training is significant in view of Florida's requirement that only six credits are needed in reading instruction for the bachelor's degree in education and only nine for the master's degree.

The project's success was demonstrated by the fact that the number of students who performed below grade level dropped, despite a 30 per cent turnover in teachers.

Right to Read Program

As stated earlier, a number of paraprofessionals are being used in reading programs outside the confines of the classroom. Indeed, many work with functionally illiterate adults whose access to facilities that will help them acquire reading skills has been limited, blocked, or nonexistent.

The Right to Read Program, a national campaign to eliminate illiteracy, serves adults as well as school-age children. In 1972 the Appalachian Adult Education Center developed Right to Read projects in Pike County, Ohio, and in Rowan and Montgomery counties, Kentucky, to serve disadvantaged adults in rural areas who could not or would not attend formal programs (Appalachian Adult Education Center, 1973). The project's outreach strategy involved six paraprofessionals (former students in adult basic education), who sought out functionally illiterate adults and delivered individualized instruction, ongoing support services, and counseling to them and reading readiness materials to their preschool children. The project's primary purpose was established in view of the following conditions: (1) the difficulty of reaching and recruiting the nation's most undereducated and deprived population—the stationary poor, (2) the target group's geographic isolation and lack of communication systems, (3) the paucity of agencies or groups that could provide supportive services to and recruit the target population into a literacy program, (4) the previous successes of teams consisting of trained paraprofessionals and professionals, (5) the critical shortage of trained educators of adults, and (6) the common notion that the poor cannot or will not take advantage of learning opportunities, even when opportunities are available.

The six paraprofessionals who participated in the projects' intensive pre- and in-service workshops were trained in reading diagnosis, individualized instruction, and methods of home instruction. Supervision and ongoing support were provided by professional educators and reading specialists.

The six paraprofessionals served 103 families, including more than 50 preschoolers. Virtually all the families recruited for the projects remained in them during 1972, and the adults who took part (ranging in ages from 16 to 67), had an average monthly gain in reading level of 0.37 years (projected yearly gain was 4.44 years.) The cost of the project per family was $394. When this figure is compared to expenditures of from $550 to $1,400 per pupil in the public schools, the Appalachian Right to Read projects' expenditures for home instruction represented a substantial saving.

Basic Literacy Program, Brooklyn House of Detention

A basic literacy program for inmates in the Brooklyn House of Detention in New York uses inmates as tutors for fellow prisoners. The initiators of this program, which is administered by the School of Continuing Education, New York City Community College, under a grant provided by the New York State Office of Crime Control Planning, hoped to reach 275 to 300 inmates (including tutors and students) by mid- 1975. To prepare for their roles, tutors attend 40 hours of in-service training delivered by professional staff of the School of Continuing Education. Each tutor then gives 14 hours of individual instruction to an inmate, stressing his strengths and life experiences as well as phonics, word and phrase recognition, vocabulary, English usage, development of comprehension skills, and oral and written communication. All classes are supervised by an education coordinator provided by the college.

The majority of tutors and students are Spanish-speaking or black; bilingual tutors are selected in proportion to the number of Spanish-speaking students.

Although evaluations of this program have been qualitative rather than quantitative, the use of inmates as tutors has created a positive, goal-directed environment within the Brooklyn House of Detention. Inmates who received tutoring on a one to one or one to two basis made substantial progress in reading in a relatively short period and when released, they were better equipped to become useful members of society.

CONCLUSION

Paraprofessionals have proved to be a valuable resource in a variety of reading programs. Because of increasing demands for high-quality education, accountability, changes in school enrollment patterns, revised curricula, and individualized instruction, the number of paraprofessionals employed in reading instruction has increased substantially. In an address to the International Reading Association, Dauzat emphasized the valuable contribution that paraprofessionals can make to reading programs and urged professionals not to "squander on nonproductive tasks the potential source of rich opportunities for children which the paraprofessional represents [1972, p. 10]." Similarly, Mauser (1972) pointed out that the issue is no longer whether paraprofessionals should be used but how to prepare and use them and tap their potential fully.

The following suggestions and recommendations will contribute to judicious use of paraprofessionals in reading programs:

1. Paraprofessionals are not merely a cheap supply of labor. Therefore, educators, school administrators, district personnel, and others must look beyond the immediate economic returns involved and carefully examine the long-range benefits of using them. Paraprofessionals are often motivated to complete their education and become local teachers. As future teachers, due to their previous training, experience, and contact with reading professionals, they will be highly qualified teachers of reading.

2. Reading programs, institutions, etc., that use paraprofessionals should be encouraged to implement built-in mechanisms for career advancement among the paraprofessional. Career lattices that differentiate job status, salaries, and job responsibilities on the basis of training, education, and life and job experiences can be used effectively for this purpose.

3. Both pre-and in-service training of reading paraprofessionals must reflect the job to be performed. If paraprofessionals are to function effectively, they must be equipped with the necessary skills, knowledge, and theoretical background to carry out their responsibilities.

4. Reading as well as other paraprofessionals must participate in pre- and in-service training sessions. Introduction of paraprofessionals into reading programs necessitates new roles for professionals. Teachers, administrators, and others must know how to utilize the paraprofessional's skills effectively and develop the necessary management, supervisory, and monitory skills.

5. Finally, educators must not lose sight of the main purpose behind the use of the reading paraprofessional: to help individuals with reading deficits improve their reading skills. Therefore, qualitative and quantitative evaluations of the paraprofessional's effect on the learner must continue.

REFERENCES

Appalachian Right to Read community based centers. Louisville, Ky.: Appalachian Adult Education Center, August 1973.

Conant, E. *A cost effectiveness study of employing non-professional teaching aides in the public schools.* Eugene: Oregon Study Council, College of Education, University of Oregon, 1971.

Dauzat, S. V. Wise utilization of human resources: The paraprofessional in the reading program. *International Reading Association Conference Papers,* 1972, **17,** 62–69.

Drije, C. *COP participants and the teaching of reading.* COP Bulletin No. 5. New York: New Careers Training Laboratory, 1974.

Gartner, A. *Paraprofessionals and their performance. A survey of education, health, and social service programs.* New York: Praeger, 1971.

Helm, P. A. program to train paraprofessionals in reading instruction. Paper presented at the National Reading Conference, Tampa, Fla., 1971.

Goralski, P., & Karl, J. Kindergarten teacher aides and reading readiness in Minneapolis public schools. *Journal of Experimental Education,* 1968, **36,** 18–27.

Lay Tutor Reading Improvement Program. Wagner, S. D., East Charles Mix Independent School District 102, July 1971.

Mauser, A. J. Why paraprofessionals in reading? Paper presented to the International Reading Association, Washington, D.C., May 1972.

National Education Association. How the professional feels about teacher aides. *National Educational Association Journal,* 1967, **56** (2), 18–21.

Rist, R. C. Black studies and paraprofessionals: A prescription for ailing reading programs in urban black schools. *Journal of Reading,* 1971, 14.

Shipp, M. Teacher aides: A survey. *National Elementary Principal,* 1967, 46, 93–98.

Sugarman, S. D. Educational consumerism through the courts. *Urban/ Rural,* 1974, **3,** 20. (Newsletter of the Urban/Rural Leadership Training Institute, Stanford, Calif.)

Veaco, L. *The effect of paraprofessional assistance on the academic achievement of migrant children.* (Doctoral dissertation, University of the Pacific, Fresno, Calif.)

Chapter 6

A DECADE OF PARAPROFESSIONAL PROGRAMS IN THE MINNEAPOLIS PUBLIC SCHOOLS

Alan Sweet

Over the past ten years, many changes and innovations that have occurred in education have affected the operation of schools. But the greatest impact on the actual instructional process has been achieved through the introduction of paraprofessionals. The very presence of another adult changes the atmosphere of the classroom. More important, it gives teachers and other staff who work with paraprofessionals the means to develop a better delivery system of educational services to students. In school systems such as the one in Minneapolis, where the emphasis has been on hiring community residents as paraprofessionals without imposing educational requirements there has been an even broader impact on the classroom and school. In addition to providing educational services, these paraprofessionals are a liaison between the community and the school and provide a different cultural input, and serve as an alternative adult model for students. They also provide a valuable link between parents and the school staff.

DEVELOPMENT

Like many school systems throughout the United States, the Minneapolis paraprofessional program was developed with funds from Title I of the Elementary and Secondary Education Act of 1965. However, two earlier experiences with paraprofessionals established the philosophy on which the program was developed. The first was initiated in the summer of 1964 by the Youth Development Project with funds from the Juvenile Delinquency and Youth Offenses Control Act and involved hiring several community persons as paraprofessionals in one target area elementary school. The second experience, a 1965 Urban Area Summer School, was funded by the Economic Opportunity Act and involved 126 paraprofessionals. This program operated in 16 elementary schools in low-income communities and contained the highest proportion of minority students. Each teacher was aided by a paraprofessional who lived in the community and qualified as a low-income family member. Teachers were involved in the selection of the paraprofessionals and efforts were made to employ parents of the students. Hiring low-income neighborhood persons with no educational requirements was a radical idea at the time and was certainly a departure from earlier experiments with paraprofessionals, which had rather high educational requirements, often a liberal arts degree. (Some paraprofessional programs still maintain similar educational requirements.)

The Urban Area Summer School proved to be a valuable learning experience. Teachers who asked "What do I do with a paraprofessional?" when summer school began were soon asking "What would I do without a paraprofessional?" The teachers' overwhelming acceptance of paraprofessionals set the stage for a paraprofessional program during the regular school year when funds under Title I became available that fall. Two hundred paraprofessionals were hired, many of whom had worked in the summer school program. Although there was no requirement to hire low-income neighborhood residents, this policy was continued, as was the involvement of teachers in the selection of paraprofessionals, who were chosen on the basis of their personal qualities after residency and need were established. In November 1965, the use of paraprofessionals was extended when home visitors, now called social work aides, were employed. These individuals were introduced under the Higher Incentive Project, also funded by Title I, and were considered adjuncts to the existing School Social Work Program. Much of their growth and development paralleled that of teacher aides. Since 1965 the increased demand for paraprofessional services plus their inclusion in the staffing of new programs has increased the number of paraprofessionals working in the Minneapolis public schools to more than 1,400.

The development of the Minneapolis paraprofessional program was enhanced considerably by the New Careers program and the Career Opportunities Program (COP). These programs not only made it possible to bring in additional personnel and provide additional training opportunities but were instrumental in establishing a career lattice, which was adopted by the Board of Education to cover all paraprofessional personnel.

The career lattice is an integral part of the entire Auxiliary Personnel Program, regardless of the funding sources, and serves as the basic structure for employment and advancement. It includes four broad categories of paraprofessionals: teacher aide, social work aide, media aide, and counselor aide. Each category contains three classifications (School Aide I, School Aide II, and School Assistant) and six salary steps. Movement from one category to another (Teacher Aide, Social Work Aide, Media Aide, and Counselor Aide) is possible at the School Aide I and II levels.

Progression on the salary steps depends on successful experience and participation in training.

When the paraprofessional program was brought under city civil service, the career lattice became the model for the classification structure. The present lattice, with its hierarchically defined tasks, selection criteria, traits and characteristics, training and transfer opportunities, and fringe benefits and salary schedule, is the current career structure of the Auxiliary Personnel Program of the Minneapolis Public Schools. Future revisions of this lattice are expected to reflect ongoing program developments.

Although the career lattice delineates job descriptions at all three classification levels in terms of general and illustrative functions and responsibilities, these descriptions are suggestive rather than regulatory. The important factor is that each paraprofessional works directly with a teacher, social worker, counselor, librarian, and so forth and that certified person has the professional freedom and responsibility to use the paraprofessional's services to provide the best possible education for students. As paraprofessionals become more proficient through experience and training, they will be involved more deeply in the instructional process and be given increased responsibilities.

When paraprofessionals were first introduced into the schools in 1965, the program objectives were to relieve the teacher of routine clerical and housekeeping tasks, to provide a liaison for the community, and to have another adult in the classroom with whom children could develop a positive relationship. With these objectives in mind, teachers began learning how to work with paraprofessionals. A weekly three-hour in-service training session for paraprofessionals was written into the program, and a full-time consultant was hired to coordinate the training and to give the program direction. During this crucial development period, teachers were encouraged to be creative, to experiment, and to share their experiences. There was little formal policy. The philosophy was to let the program grow and shape itself and to add structure when structure was needed. Workshops for teachers were conducted using as resource persons the teacher-paraprofessional teams who had most successfully worked out a meaningful role for the paraprofessional and principals who were most supportive of this role. By the end of the first year, great progress had been made in the successful utilization of paraprofessionals, but teachers were concerned about the legality of this new role. At the teachers' suggestion, a summer workshop was held to explore the legal and functional factors in the relationships between teachers, paraprofessionals, and administrators. Attorneys for the board of education worked with the group, and a policy statement was adopted in February of 1967. It contains the following section about teacher roles vis-a-vis paraprofessional roles:

> The professional teacher is trained and certified to perform certain functions in the education of children. The responsibilities that are reserved for teachers involve: (1) analyzing the instructional needs of pupils; (2) prescribing educational activities to meet the pupils' needs; and (3) certain supervisory responsibilities consistent with established school policy and directed by the school principal.
>
> Teachers working with nonprofessional helpers, either in or out of the classroom, must rely upon their own professional judgment when assigning duties to nonprofessional helpers.
>
> These duties should not infringe upon the responsibilities reserved for teachers, but nonprofessionals may assist teachers in meeting their responsibilities.
>
> The school principal retains the traditional responsibility for supervision of the school and the entire staff.

In effect, the policy states that teachers can give paraprofessionals any assignment that they, in their professional judgment, deem appropriate for that paraprofessional.

The policy statement did much to eliminate the teachers' concern that they might "go too far" in the assignments they gave paraprofessionals, and it gave them the freedom and encouragement to develop a meaningful role for paraprofessionals in education. However, teachers continued to be concerned that school administrators would replace teachers with paraprofessionals for the sake of fiscal expediency or in crisis situations. With this in mind, the superintendent asked that the policy be clarified by drafting specific rules to govern administrative action. These rules, adopted in October 1967, stated:

> 1. In the absence of the teacher, for any reason, the non-professional may not assume or be assigned the responsibilities reserved for teachers.
>
> 2. Nonprofessionals may not be given independent responsibility for classroom management and organization.
>
> 3. The nonprofessional may not function in a *normal classroom* helping role if a certified teacher is not available for direction and guidance.

These rules allowed a teacher the flexibility to leave a paraprofessional in charge during a limited absence but specifically prohibited paraprofessionals from being used as substitute teachers or strike breakers. This proved to be most significant, because in the spring of 1970 the Minneapolis teachers went on strike. The ruling was adhered to, and what could have been the source of distrust and alienation between teachers and paraprofessionals actually strengthened their relationship. Many paraprofessionals reported for work during the strike at the direction of their teachers, who knew they could ill afford to lose pay. When the strike ended, the Minneapolis Federation of Teachers gave paraprofessionals a vote of confidence by paying the income lost by any paraprofessional who had chosen not to enter the buildings.

Two additional policies related to paraprofessionals

have been adopted by the Minneapolis Board of Education. One, adopted in March 1968, dealt with the use of paraprofessionals throughout the school system rather than solely in target area schools. The other, adopted in July 1971, stated that "the Minneapolis Public Schools shall continue to employ qualified paraprofessional personnel to work under the supervision of certified professionals" and that "teachers shall have the option to be represented in the selection process for paraprofessionals." It also stated that teachers must be consulted before paraprofessionals are assigned to them and that they shall have the opportunity to be involved in evaluating them.

From the beginning, the two major teacher organizations, the Minneapolis Federation of Teachers and the Minneapolis Education Association, kept in close contact. Thus both were well informed and knew that teachers were involved in the development of the paraprofessional program. Unfortunately, another segment of the school staff was not involved or informed, and this proved to be a source of considerable difficulty when the program was brought into the civil service system. The clerical union opposed the hiring of paraprofessionals without citywide written civil service testing, and only after considerable effort on the part of both school and civil service staff was the selection process by oral testing in neighborhood schools preserved.

Although the number of paraprofessionals in the Minneapolis schools has continued to increase and the use of aides has spread throughout all areas of the school program, the basic philosophy of hiring neighborhood residents has been maintained. Applications and medical examinations are facilitated by the civil service office, but the testing and hiring is done in the individual schools by the principal or other staff. Testing consists of a basic literacy test and an interview to determine a person's desire and ability to work with children and her knowledge of the community. The usual six-month civil service probationary period applies to all newly appointed paraprofessionals. During that time, orientation and assistance is provided by an experienced aide who serves as an aide coordinator. In addition, the teacher with whom the new paraprofessional works provides training and assistance in the job assignment and does periodic evaluation. After successfully completing her probation, the paraprofessional achieves tenure.

Permanently certified paraprofessionals receive the following fringe benefits: vacation pay; sick leave; holiday pay; leave of absence for death in the immediate family, religious holidays, and jury duty; workmen's compensation; shared cost retirement; optional shared cost family hospitalization; general liability; free legal assistance in the event of work-related civil actions; and the option of leave of absence without pay. Part-time paraprofessionals, who work less than 20 hours a week, also receive these benefits, with the exception of sick leave, vacation pay, shared cost retirement, and hospitalization.

Salary increases have been granted by the board of education on the same basis as other civil service employees despite the lack of formal organization. Although two attempts were made to establish a bargaining unit for paraprofessionals, neither was successful. In 1971 the Minneapolis Association of Paraprofessionals, an affiliate of the Minnesota Education Association, petitioned the director of the Bureau of Mediation Services for recognition as a bargaining agent. An election was held late in 1971, but the resolution failed to pass. The Minneapolis Federation of Teachers filed a similar petition, but an election early in 1972 also failed to establish a bargaining agent. However, because recent state legislation has revised the requirements for establishing a bargaining unit, another attempt may be made.

TRAINING FOR PARAPROFESSIONALS

Training has been an integral part of the Minneapolis Paraprofessional Program from the beginning. Inherent in the philosophy on which the program was founded is the belief that neighborhood residents have life experiences and cultural understanding that are invaluable to professional faculty and to students. Educational background is less important because skills that are needed for a particular assignment can be acquired through training. Furthermore, training undertaken while actively working with students is more productive and meaningful.

Through the participation of the Minneapolis public schools in a New Careers program and the adoption of a New Careers philosophy, training became part of an upgrading and advancement plan that eventually became an officially adopted career lattice for all paraprofessional personnel. The training program now offers a wide variety of training opportunities and involves many different training resources. Every effort is made to provide training for specific job assignments and to meet the needs of individual paraprofessionals. Opportunities range from basic education to academic courses and are offered at community schools and college campuses. Any course that will help a paraprofessional work more effectively with teachers and students is considered legitimate training and carries credit for advancement on the career lattice. There is no hierarchy of credit; an in-service course has as much credit value as a college course; the only criterion is that courses must be relevant to the paraprofessional's assignment.

Courses designed to increase skills for working in reading and math as well as in child psychology and development have high priority. Courses developed at the request of teachers and paraprofessionals usually deal with the acquisition of skills needed for a specific function. These courses include audiovisual training, games for elementary school children, seventh-grade mathematics, sign language for the deaf, first aid, and calligraphy. Instructors are teachers, principals, supervisors, and experienced paraprofessionals from the Minneapolis schools and from any other available source. The Red Cross provides instructors in first aid, the director of a child guidance clinic teaches courses in basic child psychology and child behavior, a paraprofessional teaches beginning and advanced courses in audiovisual techniques, a former New Careerist and COP graduate teaches courses in chemical awareness. As paraprofessionals become involved in new roles through the initiation of new programs or as teachers involve them in new activities, training courses are developed to teach them the skills they need.

Paraprofessionals are encouraged to participate in training for their own personal development, as well as to help them in their work with students. Links have been established with many different training sources to provide the widest variety of courses possible. Basic education courses are available throughout the city for those who want to brush up on the basic skills or have not completed high school and want to earn a GED. Courses in efficient reading, effective writing, and word power may be taken through the educational television network. Any community school courses that are relevant to work with students or to a specific assignment are approved as appropriate paraprofessional training. Occasionally, community groups and organizations sponsor workshops that provide excellent training opportunities for paraprofessionals. Many courses in professional growth developed for Minneapolis teachers are available to paraprofessionals as well, and often provide an opportunity for the teacher and paraprofessional to learn together.

College courses are available through Metropolitan Community College and the University of Minnesota. In addition, COP participants may enroll at Augsburg College, the College of St. Catherine, and Minnesota Metropolitan State College. Many courses sponsored by Model Cities and Pilot Cities are offered in the community. A close working relationship has been developed with the Metropolitan Community College. Its regular course offerings are available to paraprofessionals and, at the request of the public schools, special courses are developed. Also, the public schools' paraprofessional training staff has developed courses that have become part of the college curriculum, and they serve as part-time community college staff to teach these courses. The titles of these courses are as follows: The Role and Function of the School Paraprofessional, The Community and Its School, Values Clarification, The Role and Function of the Community Helping Person, and Problem Solving and Teaming for School Personnel. The training staff also supervises and verifies credits for work experience earned by COP participants.

Courses at the University of Minnesota have been available for paraprofessionals since early in the program. Throughout the New Careers program and, later, COP, the university served as an educational training resource. Recently, the Minneapolis paraprofessional training staff was moved both physically and administratively to the Minneapolis Public Schools/University of Minnesota Teacher Center on the university's main campus. This move enhances both teacher and paraprofessional training.

A paraprofessional training bulletin listing available courses is distributed to all paraprofessionals before the beginning of each quarter. The paraprofessional training staff expedites registration and sends confirmations for courses requested. These courses are offered tuition free to all paraprofessionals.

NEW ROLES FOR TEACHERS

Although it is important for a paraprofessional to be well trained, it is equally important for the supervising teacher or other staff member to be trained in using the paraprofessional effectively. The most important single factor in the success of a teacher-paraprofessional team is the supervising teacher's skill in assigning and supervising the paraprofessional's activities. Working with a paraprofessional places teachers in a new role—one for which there usually has been no formal training. Instead of the traditional training and role of being exclusively responsible for the educational activities of a classroom of students, the teacher is expected to function as a supervisor, trainer, and evaluator of another adult as well. This expanded role requires additional skills. A teacher has the opportunity to spend more time with students, try different teaching techniques, and provide more individualized instruction. Because students receive more individual attention, discipline problems diminish. The classroom becomes a more interesting and exciting place for both the students and the teacher.

In spring 1974 the Minnesota Department of Education (1974), in cooperation with the Duluth and Minneapolis Career Opportunities Programs, conducted a descriptive study of the effective use of COP-trained paraprofessionals. When asked how the teacher's role has changed as a result of having a COP paraprofessional in the classroom, teachers and principals unanimously agreed that the paraprofessional enables the teacher to individualize instruction to a greater extent and to provide more individual attention to more children. A majority of teachers also said that the aide enabled them to conduct more small-group instruction. It is clear that these teachers perceive themselves as functioning differently when assisted by paraprofessionals and they indicated that their roles have been expanded to include supervisory responsibility for another adult.

The key to the successful use of a paraprofessional is that the teacher actually accepts and implements the role change. If teachers continue to teach and manage classrooms in the same manner they did before they gained the services of a paraprofessional, the overall educational impact is minimal. In fact, if a paraprofessional is used in a strictly clerical role, there is danger that the teacher will become a "paper teacher" and ultimately have even less contact with students than before. Therefore, teachers and other supervisors of paraprofessionals must be properly oriented to their new role; have the opportunity to become effective supervisors, efficient trainers, and objective evaluators; and receive the necessary guidance to develop the kind of teacher/paraprofessional team relationship that will deliver optimum educational services to students.

Teacher Orientation

First-year teachers or teachers who are new to a school that uses paraprofessionals receive an orientation before school begins to acquaint them with the philosophy of using neighborhood residents as paraprofessionals, the school's policies concerning the use of paraprofessionals, and the responsibilities of supervising a paraprofessional. Teachers who will be working with a Title I program or any other categorical program that funds paraprofessionals should also be oriented to state and federal guidelines so that they understand the program's goals and objectives and how paraprofessionals can be assigned to achieve these goals. Teachers who are skilled in the use of paraprofessionals can be a valuable resource for new teachers.

A paraprofessional can be a threat to a first-year teacher, and an experienced paraprofessional can be a threat to any teacher new to the building. Fortunately, most teachers coming into a new school regard an experienced paraprofessional as an asset rather than a threat—as a ready source of information about the community, the students, and school procedures. New teacher-paraprofessional teams should jointly share information about previous work with other teachers or aides and outline which procedures worked better than others.

The orientation workshop for teachers should focus on the new role of supervisor, trainer, and evaluator of a paraprofessional. The parameters of this new role must be discussed and the burden of responsibility emphasized. The teacher/supervisor should discuss the educational goals for the class with the paraprofessional, use professional judgment in assigning duties that are compatible with the paraprofessional's current skill and experience, and give clear and specific instructions.

Teacher orientations usually begin with a narrated slide/tape presentation titled "The School Aide Story," which explains the Minneapolis Paraprofessional Program. This presentation gives teachers background information on the program's development and funding sources and a general overview of the many different paraprofessional assignments in the schools. A supervisor's manual containing basic information about supervising paraprofessionals serves as a guide as well as a ready reference. A copy of the Career Lattice is given to each teacher and paraprofessional. This manual is especially helpful because it includes job descriptions in terms of general and illustrative functions, responsibilities, selection criteria, training opportunities, and transfer possibilities for the three paraprofessional classifications. It also describes the salary schedule and fringe benefits. Another booklet titled "Let's Talk About . . . Manual for Aides" is also distributed and discussed. It explains the personnel function of the program in detail, including hiring procedures, policies, rules and guidelines, and an outline for orienting a paraprofessional to a school. The supervisor is responsible for interpreting these policies, rules, guidelines, and procedures and for helping the paraprofesssional become acquainted with the building and fellow employees. Although teachers are the direct supervisors of paraprofessionals, they must understand that they have access to the principal and to the paraprofessional training staff for assistance if the need arises.

Another valuable aid for teachers who will be working with paraprofessionals is a narrated slide/tape presentation "So You Are an Aide." This presentation was developed to help both paraprofessionals and teachers understand some of the basic elements of being a successful paraprofessional and is especially helpful in workshops in which both teachers and paraprofessionals participate. Teachers also receive a pamphlet titled "What Supervisors Expect from Paraprofessionals and What Paraprofessionals Expect from Their Supervisors" and bookmarks with the goals of the Minneapolis Paraprofessional Program on one side and the paraprofessional's general responsibilities on the other.

More recent materials developed by the paraprofessional training staff are a self-evaluation for supervisors and a narrated slide/tape presentation called "Team Effectiveness." The former consists of a series of questions for supervisors under the main headings of "Getting Started," "Functioning as an Effective Team," and "Feedback and Evaluation." The first section focuses on the team concept, elements of an effective team, and variables that affect the team and, also, contains follow-up activities and suggestions for implementation.

Teachers as Trainers and Supervisors

The teacher must be a trainer, especially if the paraprofessional has never worked in a classroom. In fact, the training that the paraprofessional receives from the teacher is probably the most important training she will ever receive. Its importance is recognized by the fact that no additional outside training is required for advancing up the first three steps of the Career Lattice. The teacher must orient the paraprofessional to classroom procedures and the use of instructional materials, demonstrating precisely how materials will be used, if necessary. The teacher must realize that training is an ongoing process and that as the paraprofessional gains in skills and experience, her duties and involvement must increase accordingly. As they work together and the teacher becomes more skillful in directing the paraprofessional in learning activities, additional training will often enhance the team's effectiveness. The teachers should encourage paraprofessionals to participate in training opportunities that will enhance their effectiveness in the classroom.

Through regular school visits, members of the paraprofessional training staff seek suggestions for in-service courses and pass on ideas that will help develop effective teacher/paraprofessional teams. As teachers become skilled supervisors, they should be encouraged to serve as resource persons for teacher-paraprofessional workshops and paraprofessional in-service courses.

Teacher as Evaluators

The role of evaluator is sometimes difficult for a teacher. Giving positive feedback or complimenting a paraprofessional for a job well done is not difficult, but dealing with unsatisfactory performance requires the courage to face a problem and deal with it objectively. The teacher should meet privately with the paraprofessional, discuss problems openly and objectively and suggest ways for improvement. He should listen carefully to anything the paraprofessional has to say about the problem and make certain that the paraprofessional understands exactly what is expected of her. Although the emphasis should be on the positive, both positive and negative feedback are necessary if a paraprofessional is to become an effective team member. When a teacher fails to deal with a problem, the team relationship deteriorates to the point where the teacher and paraprofessional can no longer work together. If the teacher has discussed the problem with the paraprofessional and no improvement is noted, the principal and the paraprofessional training staff should be contacted for assistance. If the problem persists, the paraprofessional may work more successfully with another teacher or in some cases must be discharged.

Although some form of evaluation should be continued throughout a team's working relationship, evaluation —both formal and informal—is most important during the first few months that a teacher and paraprofessional work together. It is during this time that relationships which are crucial to the team's development are established. Frequent and thorough evaluation is also important to help the paraprofessional complete the six-month probationary period successfully and to give the teacher an adequate background for making the probationary report. Teachers should give their paraprofessional partners a copy of "Self Evaluation for Paraprofessionals" and periodically discuss the points that are appropriate at the time.

A special one-page outline serves as a general guide for evaluating a paraprofessional early in the relationship. This outline deals with the paraprofessional's personal characteristics in relation to the job, an assessment of her performance, and questions to be discussed with her. It is not a written report, yet it provides a framework in which the teacher and paraprofessional can discuss how their working relationship is developing, examine the areas in which the paraprofessional needs to improve, and formulate plans to bring about improvement.

All new paraprofessionals in the Minneapolis schools must be evaluated after three months. A detailed form is used for this purpose. The evaluation covers job performance and relationships with students, supervisors, parents, the community, and other aides; there is also a space for the paraprofessional's comments. The teacher completes the evaluation, discusses it with the paraprofessional, they both sign it, and it is sent to the district's Office of Auxiliary Personnel. If the evaluation is unsatisfactory, a member of the paraprofessional training staff will work with the team to alleviate problems and set definite plans for improvement.

When a paraprofessional approaches the end of the six-month probationary period, the supervisor completes a short civil service evaluation that determines continued employment. If the paraprofessional is performing satisfactorily, she receives tenure; if not, she is terminated. Obviously, for the sake of both team development as well as for decisions as to continued employment, consistent evaluations and feedback are essential during the first six months a teacher and paraprofessional work together. However, if the working relationship between teacher and paraprofessional is to grow, some form of regular evaluation is necessary. Teachers should provide verbal feedback whenever it is appropriate, set aside time regularly to talk over how things are going and to suggest improvements, and, if possible, conduct an annual formal evaluation. The paraprofessional training staff is currently experimenting with two different forms to assist teachers in carrying out these evaluations. One is similar to the three-month evaluation; the other is more subjective. The form that teachers find most helpful will be used.

Members of the paraprofessional training staff serve as resource persons to help teachers and paraprofessionals improve their team performance. On request, they conduct workshops for teachers and paraprofessionals separately or together. Workshops of this kind can be most effective when both teachers and paraprofessionals are included. Members of the training staff spend much of their time in schools talking with principals, teachers, and other profes-

sional staff and with paraprofessionals about both successful and problem areas and how the use of paraprofessionals
can be improved or replicated. They investigate current
needs for training and solicit ideas for new courses. Regular contact with school staff is essential, not only to provide
service to teams, but to help the training staff keep up to
date through direct contact with practitioners, maintain a
realistic attitude by dealing with ongoing team development, and provide the background necessary to keep the
training program responsive to current needs.

Although this discussion has focused primarily on
teachers as supervisors of paraprofessionals, the same basic
principles apply to others who work with paraprofessionals.
School social workers, counselors, and librarians who work
with paraprofessionals also find that their roles have expanded—that they now have the opportunity to perform at
a higher level of professional competence. They too have
become supervisors, trainers, and evaluators of other
adults. Developing a good team relationship is equally important for them. Most of the materials discussed in this
chapter, especially the Career Lattice and "Let's Talk
About . . . Manual for Aides," were developed for use by all
supervisors of paraprofessionals.

IIMPACT OF PARAPROFESSIONALS

Paraprofessionals are an integral part of the Minneapolis
public schools. They have contributed much to the education of students and staff and to good school-community
relations. Their work has also been valuable for them because it has provided meaningful employment with an opportunity for training and advancement. Working with
teachers and other school staff to help students has contributed to their own personal growth. Success as a paraprofessional and additional education through the training

program have helped many develop greater self-esteem. In many cases, participation in training has had a positive effect on the educational attitudes and aspirations of the paraprofessionals' children. Working as a paraprofessional has also been an avenue to other employment. The same work experience and training that advances them on the Career Lattice makes them desirable employees in other kinds of jobs as well.

New Careers and COP have provided many low-income paraprofessionals with additional educational opportunities. Many have advanced to the upper levels of the Career Lattice, and more than 50 have earned college degrees. Many graduates are now teachers or social workers in the Minneapolis public schools. Some are working in other school systems or social agencies.

As in other school districts that developed paraprofessional programs, it became apparent that all paraprofessionals had much to gain in meeting to share ideas and participate in workshops together. With this in mind, the Minneapolis paraprofessional training staff, with the cooperation of staff and paraprofessionals in St. Paul, Duluth, and other school systems, decided to organize a statewide conference. With assistance from the Minnesota Department of Education and with financial support and publicity from both the Minnesota Education Association and the Minnesota Federation of Teachers, the first Minnesota Statewide Conference for Teacher Aides was held in Minneapolis in late 1972. This conference, as well as those in 1973 and 1974, featured a variety of workshops of interest to paraprofessionals and provided them with an opportunity to meet and share ideas. The 1974 conference was especially significant because it was planned and conducted by paraprofessionals, who have continued this leadership in subsequent years.

The fact that paraprofessionals have an important impact on the instructional process, the role of the teacher, and on school-community relations is well documented. So is the fact that they have a considerable amount of contact with students and that schools are a better place for children because of them. However, little has been done to substantiate their impact on how much students actually learn. Citywide testing shows that reading achievement in the Minneapolis schools has increased in consecutive years, and paraprofessionals are deeply involved in reading programs. But how much and in what ways they have contributed to this improvement is unknown. A study on the paraprofessional's role in the elementary classroom notes the emphasis on paraprofessional involvement with the cognitive and emotional development of children but does not describe the results of this involvement. Another study describes in detail the amount of time a paraprofessional in social work spends with students, parents, staff, and agencies as well as on routine activities. But like the first study, it does not attempt to assess the effects of their efforts on students.

A study on the use of COP-trained paraprofessionals conducted by the Minnesota Department of Education found that although most teachers, social workers, and principals talked about the increased individual attention that paraprofessionals provide for students, less than half stated that children learn more because of their services. A majority did agree that paraprofessionals have a positive effect on students' attitudes toward school and that students' self-concepts are improved because of the increased individual attention and help provided by COP paraprofessionals. The only research that measured the actual impact of paraprofessionals in the Minneapolis Public Schools showed that students in kindergarten classrooms where paraprofessionals were present gained significantly more in reading readiness than those in classrooms without paraprofessionals. Research findings such as this, which indicate that paraprofessionals do have a measurable positive effect on student performance are helpful in developing greater use of paraprofessionals in schools. But perhaps the most important influence is the continual clamor on the part of school staffs for paraprofessional help.

The growth of the Minneapolis Paraprofessional Program is related, in large part, to the school administration's commitment to use paraprofessionals. Although an increase in federal and state funds has contributed to this growth, a substantial portion of the program is supported by local tax funds. In addition to this numerical growth, new roles for paraprofessionals have been developed. For example, the basic skills centers for improving the reading skills of low achievers offer a great many paraprofessional services; the Student Aide Program uses high school students to tutor elementary school children, and the program is supervised by a former New Careerist paraprofessional in one area and by a COP participant in another. Paraprofessionals in social work are an integral part of the Student Support Program. These paraprofessionals are assigned a group of students and, under the supervision of a school social worker, make home visits, serve as advocates for students, and provide group counseling in an effort to prevent dropouts. The Minneapolis Indian Education Project has a staff of Indian school-community social work paraprofessionals who help the schools meet the needs of Indian students, work on attendance problems, and aid Indian families in their relationship with schools and social agencies.

The Minneapolis public schools are now involved in major decentralization and desegregation-integration efforts. Some schools have been paired; others have been reorganized into clusters or complexes. Alternative models of education are available to students from anywhere within the decentralized areas. Many programs involve busing. Paraprofessionals are a part of these efforts. They have moved along with the students. When educational alternatives for children are involved, paraprofessionals can choose from among a number of alternatives. Neighborhood residents who serve as desegregation counselor aides ride the buses with students to and from school. They serve a parental role, provide a familiar face, and bring community input along with the students. They work with school personnel, parents, and students to make the adjustment to the desegregation-integration plan as easy as possible. The smoothness with which the plan was implemented is a tribute to both the professional and paraprofessional staff.

The uninitiated may believe that paraprofessionals make a teacher's job easier. They do not; they should not. The duties a paraprofessional assumes release the teacher to initiate activities at a higher and broader professional level. As a result, the teacher-paraprofessional team provides a better learning environment. Using the paraprofessional in education enables schools and communities to work together to provide a better delivery system of educational services to their students.

Chapter 7

THE PARAPROFESSIONAL AS A MEMBER OF THE COLLEGE GUIDANCE TEAM

Ursula Delworth
and William F. Brown

In the 1960s students took a hard look at their colleges and universities and found them wanting in most respects. They particularly protested the lack of opportunities for student input into decision-making concerning the programs and services offered to them and into the role that the institution should play in the larger political world. Students insisted on dragging academia into the "real world" through their demonstrations and protests, by setting up alternative programs and services, and by becoming involved on a massive scale in local and national politics.

By the early 1970s, a sizable number of faculty, administrators, and staff began to realize the multiple ways in which they were failing the mainstream student—to say nothing of specific populations such as marginal students, ethnic minorities, and women. Colleges had almost uniformly dropped their *en loco parentis* role and were committed, at least on paper, to treating students as adults.

Students generally had established firm control over their own student governments and fees; were often living in coed residence halls with unrestricted hours; were present, too often as tokens, on important college committees; and in many cases were becoming "pros" in offering legal, sex, and drug counseling to their peers through student-initiated programs.

New academic and service programs evolved as students, faculty, and administrators began to work together again in the late sixties and early seventies. Many students became involved in community field work through the Peace Corp, VISTA, and other programs. More students than ever before became undergraduate teaching assistants. The idea of the campus as community, with implications for preventive work with students, gained a good deal of lip service, if not actual implementation.

Yet it was also in the early seventies—when perhaps this awareness on all sides was most heightened and commitment renewed—that higher education encountered another kind of difficulty. Questions and attacks from legislatures and governing boards reflected the public's disenchantment. Government grants dried up in many areas. Students began to find alternatives to college, and enrollments threatened to drop drastically. Now, every budget is scrutinized and subject to drastic cuts. Entire programs are being cut or eliminated, and the number of staff positions has been frozen or cut back. Consequently, students, administrators, faculty, and staff are increasingly frustrated as they attempt to improve and expand programs and services. Maintaining these programs and services at the current level has become a serious problem for many institutions.

There is no one solution to these difficulties, as numerous commissions and reports have demonstrated. Problems in funding, implementing viable education programs, and providing specific populations with access to higher education will not be solved without the large-scale commitment of many segments of society.

However, one small part of the problem of maintaining and improving services is being solved on a number of campuses as higher education turns to the use of students and other nonprofessionals as co-workers. These paraprofessional programs are frequently an expansion of the student-initiated legal, sex, and drug abuse counseling of the sixties. In addition, these programs often reflect new attempts to meet the needs of nontraditional students such as mature women, in whom colleges currently have a large investment in attracting and retaining.

THE PARAPROFESSIONAL ON CAMPUS

Who is the paraprofessional? The term has been used in the past few years to include everyone from the untrained student who volunteers to show new students around campus to persons with bachelor's degrees who undergo additional training to become paraprofessionals. In other words, the term paraprofessional is about as definitive today as is the word professional.

In this discussion of paraprofessionals on the college campus, the paraprofessional will be defined as a person who lacks extended professional training or professional credentials and is selected, trained, and given ongoing supervision to perform some specific functions that are generally performed by a professional. This does not include support services such as clerical work. True paraprofessionals must be involved in the central activities of the agency with which they are associated: e.g., counseling, advising, teaching. Although paraprofessionals are usually paid for their work, they can be volunteers if their positions meet the requirements outlined in the above definition.

The paraprofessional is most often a member of the population being served. Therefore, in higher education, he or she is a student, either undergraduate or graduate. A few programs, however, also use some nonstudents as paraprofessionals.

The use of paraprofessionals contributes to services on campus in three basic ways:

1.   Paraprofessionals permit the expansion of existing services at reduced cost because they release professionals for other duties.
2.   Paraprofessionals often bring special skills or expertise that professionals do not possess. This leads to more effective and expanded services. If the paraprofessional is a student, he or she has the asset of identification with the needs and problems of the students whom he serves.
3.   Student paraprofessionals can provide regular, systematic input into the system from the population being served concerning needs and services.

Most colleges and universities are organized into three main functioning entities: academic departments, student services, and financial affairs. Each unit has its own administration, which is responsible to the president of the college. The academic departments are organized in terms of subject areas and their faculties provide courses to students. In four-year colleges, most academic counseling is done by faculty. The second unit, student services, provides a variety of programs and services to students and sometimes to faculty as well. These services generally include personal, educational, and vocational counseling; orientation of new students; health services; housing; discipline; and (in most junior or community colleges) academic counseling. This unit may also be responsible for admissions and records, the library, athletics, and campus security. The financial affairs unit handles the institution's business affairs.

At present paraprofessionals are seldom involved in financial affairs. Many paraprofessionals work in the academic area as teaching assistants, lab instructors, or academic counseling assistants. The large majority, however, currently work in student services in the following areas:

Housing. Student paraprofessionals serve as assistants in residence halls, providing services such as information, crisis intervention, and program coordination to other students—usually freshmen. Housing paraprofessionals may also help students with problems related to off-campus housing.

Counseling. Paraprofessionals help provide services such as crisis intervention, drug counseling, and birth control. They often work with professionals to help students develop interpersonal and communications skills, plan their careers, and reduce their anxiety. In some settings they also offer individual and group counseling.

Orientation. Students have traditionally had a large amount of input into orientation programs for new students. Using a paraprofessional model, such students are now often trained to offer more specific information and advice to students during the orientation period.

Academic assistance. Paraprofessionals offer assistance in study skills and training, tutoring, and advising on academic-related matters to students.

Special or nontraditional student groups. A number of campuses have implemented paraprofessional programs to deal with the needs of nontraditional students in higher education, for example, ethnic minority students, mature women returning to campus, or physically handicapped students.

Research. Either in conjunction with the other services listed or as a separate component, paraprofessionals gather data on student needs and students' perceptions of current services.

The range of possible functions that paraprofessionals can perform in student services can be determined through the Dimensions of Counseling model developed by Morrill, Oetting, and Hurst (1974) (see Figure 7.1). This model represents one way to identify and classify a variety of helping programs or interventions that both professionals and paraprofessionals can provide. It defines programs and services along three dimensions that essentially delineate the targets of the intervention, the purpose of the intervention, and who will carry it out. The first dimension, *target of intervention,* refers to interventions aimed at the individuals, their primary group, their associational groups, or the institutional or social groups that influence their behavior. The second, *purpose of the intervention,* refers to the purpose of the intervention: i.e., is it remedial, preventive, or developmental? The third dimension is the *method of intervention,* direct or indirect. In other words, is the counselor directly involved in initiating and implementing the intervention; indirectly involved, as in consultation and training of other paraprofessionals, or indirectly involved through the use of media?

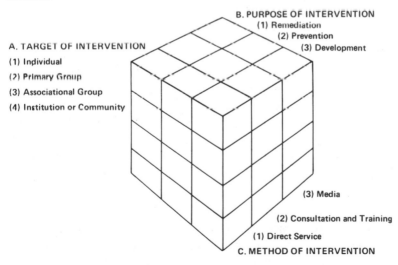

FIGURE 7.1   Dimensions of Counseling

Paraprofessionals can provide services to any of the four target groups and have a remedial, developmental, or preventative purpose for doing so. For example, a paraprofessional working on drug problems would generally be offering services to an individual with a remedial purpose. The method to be used would be indirect, assuming that the paraprofessional is supervised by a professional. A paraprofessional involved in implementing a support group for mature women returning to campus would have an individual and associational group target and generally a developmental (and possibly preventive) purpose. Again, the method would be indirect.

Analysis of current services with models such as this can help agencies decide what the priorities of service are and the areas in which paraprofessionals might be used most profitably.

RESEARCH AND SUPPORT FOR PARAPROFESSIONAL PROGRAMS

Although the use of paraprofessionals is now gaining wide support on campus, in the past colleges generally had a more cautious approach to the use of paraprofessionals than did hospitals, clinics, and community agencies. The initial policy of the American Personnel and Guidance Association (1967) was to restrict paraprofessionals to clerical assistance activities such as gathering and processing occupational information, administering and scoring routine standardized tests, and performing other subfunctions of the counselor's role. As research studies have grown in number and as professional support for the paraprofessional movement on campus has increased, the association has adopted a more receptive policy (see Delworth, Sherwood & Casaburri, 1974; Guidance and Counseling Staff, 1973; and Zimpfer, 1973).

Studies by Crane and Anderson (1971) and Geer (1971) have found solid support among college administrators. Paraprofessional tasks most favored by administrators in both surveys were tutoring, freshmen orientation, help with study problems, routine testing, research aid, emergency telephone services, and counseling students who had difficulties in adjusting to college. McCarthy (1970) proposed the use of juniors and seniors in selected counseling situations on campus, and Walz (1970) described services that the student paraprofessional can offer, including college readiness programs, a student ombudsman office, and a student-staffed counseling center.

Summary of Research Studies

Although a number of research studies have been published since the early 1970s on the effectiveness of paraprofessionals in campus programs, few have compared experimental and control samples, used both pre- and postassessment, or employed objective rather than subjective criteria. Furthermore, they are dissimilar in terms of selection, training, and use of paraprofessionals. The following studies are examples of the work being done in evaluation effectiveness of paraprofessionals.

Wolff (1969) demonstrated that group experiences led by undergraduate dormitory advisers and graduate students in psychology could improve the interpersonal functioning of first-year students on a variety of measures of interpersonal behavior. Members of groups led by graduate students showed slightly more improvement than those led by dormitory advisers.

Miller and Wiegleb (1974) evaluated the Peer Help Center at Carnegie-Mellon University in terms of a variety of criteria, including an analysis of annual statistics and a survey of faculty and student knowledge of and reaction to the center. Results showed that approximately 6 per cent of the student population used the center and that the majority of students came to the center to talk with someone, usually about an interpersonal problem. Seventy-four per cent of the students in the sample reflected adequate knowledge of the center, while only 32 per cent of the faculty reflected adequate knowledge of it. The center was the students' first choice for birth control information and their second choice for help when a friend was "freaking out."

When Upcraft (1971) surveyed faculty, freshmen, and paraprofessional advisers about the effectiveness of undergraduates as advisers to freshmen, he found that in general they had positive attitudes. Freshmen rated the student advisers highest on the following items: "Was available to me when I reeded him/her" (84 per cent satisfaction), "Provided me with someone who was a friend and confidant" (74 per cent satisfaction), and "Helped me individualize and personalize my educational experience" (73 per cent satisfaction).

Smith (1974) studied students' preferences for peer counselors and found that students most often preferred a fellow student to help them with a social problem and least often to help them with a vocational problem. Approximately 20 per cent said they would not seek a fellow student for help with any problem. Students who were 26 years of age or older, married, seniors, or religiously oriented tended to agree that a university should use a students-helping-students model; others were undecided.

Other investigators made the following discoveries: Student advisers were more effective than faculty advisers in the academic area but not in the social area (Murry, 1972). Peers dealt more effectively than did professionals with problems involving social adjustment, particularly with minority students (Pyle & Snyder, 1971), and peers were effective with students from similar ethnic and socioeconomic backgrounds (Ware & Gold, 1970, 1971). Archer

(1972) trained undergraduate paraprofessionals to lead interpersonal/communication skills training groups. Shook (1960) reported that students who worked as full members of a college admissions committee provided invaluable assistance in reviewing applications. A student-operated crisis center that was established to provide a centralized information directory and referral service and ancillary services to existing agencies and facilities produced good results (McCarthy & Berman, 1971).

Although these and similar studies cannot completely validate the effectiveness of paraprofessionals, they collectively provide compelling evidence that paraprofessionals can play a valuable role in offering services to students on the college campus.

Two Additional Studies

Although many of the studies described so far exhibit serious design deficiencies, a series of investigations conducted by Brown (1965, 1972) was carefully designed to meet the basic requirements of valid scientific inquiry. Conducted over a 15-year period, this research program used college students as paraprofessionals in academic adjustment programs on several college campuses. In his initial investigation, Brown matched 216 first-year students in an experimental (counseled) sample with 216 students in a control (uncounseled) sample according to five dependent variables. Experimental subjects were organized into 54 counselee groups of four members each. Each group was carefully matched. Six paraprofessional counselors, three males and three females, received 40 hours of intensive training and then were randomly assigned to provide academic adjustment counseling for counselee groups whose members were of the same sex as the counselor. Comparisons of test-retest assessments of study skills and academic attitudes showed that the average gain scores among members of the experimental group were significantly higher than among members of the control group. The experimental group also earned grades averaging half a letter grade and 8.3 quality points higher during the first semester. Finally, anonymous replies to a questionnaire indicated that the experimental group's reactions to all evaluated aspects of the paraprofessional counseling was overwhelmingly positive.

In a follow-up study (Zunker and Brown, 1966), four professional and eight paraprofessional counselors completed identical 40-hour training programs, used identical testing and counseling materials, followed identical counseling activity sequences, and used equivalent counseling facilities. A sample of 160 freshmen, 80 males and 80 females, received academic adjustment counseling from professional counselors of the same sex. Paraprofessional counselors gave equivalent counseling to all other freshmen, and matching samples were subsequently drawn from the male freshmen who received student-to-student counseling. Test, questionnaire, and scholarship data indicated that the paraprofessional counselors were as effective as the professional counselors. Furthermore, the students who were counseled by paraprofessionals made significantly greater use of the information they received, as reflected by first-semester grades and residual study problems. Finally, the students' responses clearly revealed that those who had been counseled by their peers were more satisfied with the counseling they had received.

In a third investigation (Brown, Wehe, Haslam & Zunker, 1971), the paraprofessional counselors provided academic adjustment counseling to 124 freshmen identified as potential dropouts. Subsequently, 111 of these students were individually matched with a control group of 111 potential dropouts who had not received counseling. When the two groups were compared according to indexes of counseling outcome, the experimental group scored significantly higher on all four criteria. The uncounseled students received 41.3 per cent more unsatisfactory grade reports than did the counseled students. Furthermore, anonymous replies to a questionnaire indicated that the counselees' reactions to the student-counseling-student approach were decisively positive.

In later investigations, Brown (1972) extended the use of paraprofessionals to provide career counseling, educational advice, developmental reading, and study skills training. In each instance, test-retest results, questionnaire responses, and data on academic achievement confirmed the effectiveness of the paraprofessionals' counseling. The consistent results that Brown and his colleagues obtained indicated that paraprofessional counseling was an effective, acceptable, practical, and adaptable procedure, whether the goal of the counseling effort was the prevention or correction of academic difficulties, whether the counselees were from affluent or disadvantaged backgrounds, or whether the focus was on the typical problems of commuter or residential students.

Discussion

Although McArthur (1970) and others have warned that the research design of most studies is faulty because independent variables are not isolated and the Hawthorne effect is not controlled, offhand dismissal of the paraprofessional's contribution is untenable when set against the numerous positive reports published since 1965. Rather than reject the findings, researchers should analyze the pertinent variables in an effort to understand why paraprofessionals are effective. Carkhuff (1969) pointed out the paraprofessionals in these studies may have been effective because those who were selected were innately more health-engendering than were professional counselors. Most paraprofessional programs have systematically attempted to select individuals who have good interpersonal skills and an ability to relate well with a variety of persons. By contrast, the selection process for professionals is typically dominated by highly intellectual indexes, which may or may not correlate with effective interpersonal functioning.

The training of the two groups also tends to differ. Paraprofessional programs generally attempt to use the little time that is available to develop in the trainee the communicative and facilitative skills that will improve the functioning of persons who receive the services. Professional training programs often seem to devote the most time to developing a trainee's discriminative skills through a complex mixture of science, art, research, and practice, with little common focus to pull the training together.

PROGRAM DEVELOPMENT

A review of the research indicates overall support for paraprofessional programs. Nevertheless, a number of new programs each year never get off the ground, and some established programs founder after a sound start. Successfully sustained programs follow a developmental procedure based on evaluations that allow for both a solid basis and ongoing change. This procedure can be divided into the following components: assessment, planning and organization, selection, training, and evaluation.

Assessment

To move ahead with a paraprofessional program, campus agencies should be able to give affirmative answers to the following questions:

1.   *What is the need for a paraprofessional program?* A need must exist that can be met by paraprofessionals, either

alone or in conjunction with professionals. Paraprofessionals can be used to help maintain or expand current services, extend the agency's work into new areas, or assess students' needs and perceptions. In any case, the decision to use paraprofessionals must be based on a careful assessment of the need for their services. Part of this assessment should include an exploration of whether clients and professionals will accept the idea that paraprofessionals can perform needed services.

2.   *What support does the program have?* Regardless of how a paraprofessional program originates, the following groups must be willing to support it to some degree: prospective paraprofessionals, potential recipients of their services, professionals in the agency, agency administrators, and the college administration. Although these groups may not be equally supportive, a program will encounter great difficulty unless all of them express some interest and support. The professionals in the agency are the key group and can easily cause the program to fail unless at least a few actively support the program and are willing to work with it. Ideally, other professionals will accept the program as part of the agency, whether or not they actively support it.

3.   *What resources can the agency commit to the program?* The following resources are necessary for a paraprofessional program: (1) professional staff to plan, select, train, supervise, and evaluate, (2) secretarial and clerical assistance, (3) physical facilities such as offices, furniture, phones, and audiovisual equipment, (4) funds for salaries (if the paraprofessionals are to be paid for their work), and (5) funds for developing or acquiring the necessary testing, counseling, and teaching materials. Because all the required resources may not be available within the agency, it may be necessary to explore whether other agencies, either on or off campus, can provide them.

4.   *What benefits will accrue to the agency and the paraprofessional as a result of the program?* A well-planned and imple-

mented program should result in maintaining or expanding services. The agency should be able to specify the expected benefits of the program in concrete terms. That is, what services do staff members view as being maintained or expanded as a result of the program? To what extent? Will the benefits be offset by the resources needed to select, train, and supervise paraprofessionals? When can the agency expect to see these benefits? Many agencies find that the work involved in starting a paraprofessional program offsets the benefits for as long as a year after the program begins.

Paraprofessionals, too, must benefit from the program if they are to continue offering their services. The agency should decide what potential benefits paraprofessionals need and want and which ones the agency can provide. Some common benefits for paraprofessionals include (1) increased competence in specific skills, (2) the opportunity to explore a role in a helping profession before choosing such a field as a career, (3) the opportunity to gain experience that will facilitate admittance to graduate school or employment in a human service agency, (4) an increased feeling of self-worth and confidence, (5) satisfaction in becoming involved and being able to help bring about improved services, (6) increased contact with key persons in the campus community, and (7) money or college credit. Each potential benefit requires specific planning to become a reality. Nothing happens automatically in a paraprofessional program.

Careful and thorough assessment will help the agency decide whether to pursue the paraprofessional program. It will also aid in determining the size of the initial program. If resources and support are limited and needs are not fully documented, an agency is probably wise to limit the program at the beginning. This may mean using only two to six paraprofessionals in no more than two service areas. Then, if the evaluation is positive and if support and resources grow, the program can be expanded.

Planning and Organization

Systematic planning and organization is an ongoing process in a paraprofessional program. A number of key decisions must be made before a program begins. Each
decision, however, will require reexamination and possible
change as the program evolves and grows.

Job descriptions should be written for each paraprofessional or group of paraprofessionals, if more than one will
be performing the same task. Each job should involve the
paraprofessional as an integral part of a central function of
the agency. Paraprofessionals tend to need structure at the
beginning, and there is generally less tension when both
professionals and paraprofessionals understand clearly
what the paraprofessionals will be doing. As paraprofessionals change and grow in interests and skills, the descriptions should be rewritten to reflect their current tasks and
activities.

Professional and clerical staff need time to explore their
reactions to the program so that any anticipated problems
can be worked out. Agency administrators should insure
that these employees receive ongoing support concerning
their work with paraprofessionals.

Paraprofessionals' involvement in the day-to-day decisions
and life of the agency should be carefully planned. This
includes making provisions for paraprofessionals to get together and build their own sense of "community"; it also
includes specific plans to build in benefits for them. Many
programs report that paraprofessionals in new programs
are most concerned about improving their own skills and
competence and obtaining the physical facilities and support necessary to do their work. However, second-genera-
tion paraprofessionals tend to be more concerned about
their input into agency decisions and their impact on
agency services and organizations. Thus agencies should
plan ahead to meet these contingencies.

Funding for paraprofessionals' salaries and related expenditures must be provided on an ongoing basis as the program expands or as original sources dry up. The agency or other institutional source, work-study programs, government agencies or private foundations, and local service organizations are common funding sources for campus programs.

Plans for implementing the program's selection criteria, training design, and supervision procedures should be made to assure efficient, realistic, and coordinated program operation, and plans for evaluating the paraprofessionals and implementing the programs and services in which they will be involved should be tentatively outlined at least.

Selection of Paraprofessionals

Once the jobs to be filled are determined and described, the agency can select paraprofessionals and the professionals who will work with them.

Recruitment of paraprofessionals should be based on advertising whenever feasible, and the advertising should concentrate on target groups that planners wish to include in the program.

Qualifications include general qualities that are desirable in all paraprofessionals and specific qualifications that are necessary for each position. General qualifications usually include characteristics such as (1) sufficient interpersonal competence and communication skills to interact effectively with a variety of individuals and groups, (2) an understanding of the culture in which he will be working, (3) the ability to deal with ambiguity and stress to some extent, (4) ability to understand and work within the agency's philosophy and organization, (5) a willingness to accept standards of ethical conduct such as the confidentiality of information, and (6) the ability to organize his own daily life to a satisfactory extent.

Procedures for selecting paraprofessionals should be designed to assess as many areas as possible. The main focus should be on the qualities that are most important to the agency. Agencies often select paraprofessionals based on assessments of some combination of the following: individual interviews, resumes and references, role-playing or simulation, interpersonal communication skills (using scales such as the one developed by Carkhuff, 1969), group interviews, with one or two interviewers and as many as six applicants, and training experience.

The choice of procedures will depend on the qualities to be assessed—and often on the number of applicants. Some agencies use screening procedures to select the most promising applicants and then rely on another set of procedures to gather more in-depth information from them. Short-term training is a method of selection that makes it possible to evaluate an applicant in terms of skills, attitudes, and abilities to function effectively on a day-to-day basis. In an ongoing program, paraprofessionals should play an active role in selecting new paraprofessionals.

Selection of Professionals

Careful selection of professionals within the agency to work with paraprofessionals is a crucial and often neglected process. Generally, professionals who are capable of training and supervising paraprofessionals are mature individuals who are (1) interested in working with paraprofessionals and are extremely competent in one or more specific areas, (2) have good work habits and are self-disciplined, (3) are flexible and secure enough to learn new skills, accept feedback from paraprofessionals, and be genuinely pleased when well-trained paraprofessionals can perform certain tasks better than they can, and (4) are skilled in one or more of these following areas: selection procedures, training methodology, evaluation, and obtaining funds.

Training

Three decisions must be made early in planning a training program. What skills, attitudes and procedures will comprise the training process and content? What training methods and procedures will be used? How much preservice training will paraprofessionals need before they can begin to offer services, and how much in-service training will they receive while actively involved in agency programs?

Good training usually consists of two components: general or core training and position-specific training. Core training focuses on knowledge, skills, and attitudes considered necessary for all paraprofessionals and often covers the following topics: the policies, procedures, and organization of the agency; ethical issues such as confidentiality; "community building," i.e., learning how to use other paraprofessionals as consultants and for support; and interpersonal skills. Training in interpersonal skills is extremely important because helping, indeed, can be for better or for worse, and minimum skill is vital when attending to the person being helped, listening empathically, and communicating concretely and respectfully.

Core and position-specific training often rely on a basic model with the following components, especially in the teaching of specific skills: (1) explanation of the skill, (2) demonstration of the skill, (3) practice of the skill with feedback in the training sessions until minimum competence is achieved, and (4) practice of the skill with supervision in an actual work situation.

Interpersonal skills are often taught using Microcounseling (Ivey, 1971), Human Relations Training (Carkhuff, 1969), Interpersonal Process Recall (Kagan, 1972), or Basic Helping Skills (Danish & Hauer, 1973). Each method uses a systematic procedure and supplementary materials.

Time of training depends on how much paraprofessionals need to know before they can actually begin work in the agency. Many programs provide a minimum amount of preservice training to involve paraprofessionals as quickly as possible in the agency's work. This can usually be accomplished quite easily if the work required allows paraprofessionals to begin their tasks as they are learning the more complex or advanced skills needed for other portions of their work. However, this is impossible in programs such as "hotlines" because there is no guarantee that the problem presented will be an easy one. Therefore, the paraprofessional should be prepared to deal effectively with most problems before he or she answers the phone.

In any case, in-service training, coupled with regular supervision by and consultation with professional staff will allow paraprofessionals to develop their skills and understand their strengths and limitations.

More and more programs are utilizing advanced paraprofessionals as trainers and, in some cases, supervisors of new paraprofessionals. This buddy-system approach allows advanced paraprofessionals to learn and use new skills and provides novice paraprofessionals with models of effective paraprofessional functioning.

Evaluation

A systematic, ongoing evaluation process has four main purposes: (1) to provide feedback on performance to both paraprofessionals and professionals, (2) to determine whether specific training or service goals have been attained, (3) to help the agency decide which paraprofessional services merit continued support, and (4) to increase the program's credibility within the academic community and among top administrators.

To achieve these purposes, it is necessary to make some assessment of each component of the program development system: i.e., planning, organization, selection, and training. It is also important to evaluate the services that paraprofessionals are offering. Some programs have been able to compare the effectiveness of a service offered by paraprofessionals against the same service offered by professionals, both in terms of outcome and the recipient's satisfaction. This is a strong evaluation process, which—if positive results are obtained—should give the agency confidence in the paraprofessional program. It is also important here to examine the differences between those who receive the service (experimental group) and a group that desires the service but does not receive it immediately (control group) to determine whether the service is valuable, regardless of who provides it. Because operations such as hotlines pose problems for this type of well-controlled evaluation, they must rely on procedures that approximate this methodology.

The results of evaluation should be communicated to paraprofessionals, professionals, and administrators in terms they can understand. In many programs, it is especially difficult to communicate results to administrators; yet this is often crucial in terms of continued support and funding. Thus the program staff may have to rely on trial and error to determine what areas of the program administrators are most interested in and then present evaluation results in these areas in a manner that is acceptable to administrators.

SUMMARY

Paraprofessionals, usually students, are being used widely in higher education to maintain and expand existing services, to develop and extend new services, and to provide input into agencies in terms of needed programs. Research indicates that paraprofessionals can provide services effectively but that systematic and focused selection and training is needed if paraprofessionals are to achieve maximum effectiveness.

Although professional support for the paraprofessional movement on campus is growing steadily, considerable resistance still exists. Thus the interaction of professional and paraprofessional roles is one area that needs more attention.

Another urgent question concerns the amount and type of training and supervision that will produce maximal effectiveness. A related issue deals with how widely paraprofessionals should be trained and used. As of the mid-1970s, most training beyond core skills prepared paraprofessionals to facilitate student development in only one specific situation.

A third area that needs further exploration concerns the number and type of controls that should be imposed on paraprofessionals. The organizational and legal implications of this question are only now beginning to be addressed in higher education. Another question is whether the paraprofessional movement can earn a permanent home in academia. Despite the proliferation of programs, many are undersupported and undervalued, and many have existed for only a short time. And finally, there is the issue of whether services offered by paraprofessionals will prove effective on a long-term basis and be accepted as an important part of the mix of services available to students on campus. In other words, the future of the paraprofessional movement in higher education is not yet assured.

REFERENCES

American Personnel and Guidance Association. Support personnel for the counselor: their technical and non-technical roles and preparation. *Personnel and Guidance Journal,* 1967, **45,** 857–861.

Archer, J. Undergraduates as paraprofessional leaders of interpersonal communication skills training groups. *Dissertation Abstracts,* 1972, **32** (8), 4932.

Brown, W. F. *Student-to-student counseling.* Austin: University of Texas Press, 1972.

Brown, W. F. Student-to-student counseling for academic adjustment. *Personnel and Guidance Journal,* 1965, **43,** 811–817.

Brown, W. F., Wehe, N. O., Haslam, W. L., & Zunker, V. G. Effectiveness of student-to-student counseling on the academic adjustment of potential college dropouts. *Journal of Educational Psychology,* 1971, **64,** 285–289.

Carkhuff, R. R. *Helping and human relations,* Vols. 1 & 2. New York: Holt, Rinehart & Winston, 1969.

Crane, J. K., & Anderson, W. *College counseling directors' attitudes concerning the use of paraprofessionals.* Testing and Counseling Service Report. Columbia: University of Missouri, 1971.

Danish, S. J., & Hauer, A. L. *Helping skills: a basic training program.* New York: Behavioral Publications, 1973.

Delworth, U., Sherwood, G., & Casaburri, N. *Student paraprofessionals: A working model for higher education.* APGA Student Personnel Series No. 17. Washington, D.C.: APGA Press, 1974.

Geer, C. The paraprofessional—a panacea or a problem? Fort Collins: Colorado State University, 1971.

Guidance and Counseling Staff, North Texas State University. *Preparation of guidance associates and professional counselors within the framework of a competency-based program.* Washington, D.C.: APGA Press, 1973.

Ivey, A. E. *Microcounseling: Innovations in interviewing training.* Springfield, Ill.: Charles C Thomas, 1971.

Kagan, N. *Influencing human interaction.* East Lansing: Michigan State University Press, 1972.

McArthur, C. C. Comment on "effectiveness of counselors and counselor aides." *Journal of Counseling Psychology,* 1970, **17**, 335–336.

McCarthy, B. W. New approaches to mental health services in colleges and universities. *Psychological Reports,* 1970, **27**, 420–422.

McCarthy, B. W., & Berman, A. L. A student-operated crisis center. *Personnel and Guidance Journal,* 1971, **49**(7), 523–528.

Miller, M., & Wiegleb, C. *Evaluation of a peer help center.* Pittsburgh: Carnegie-Mellon University Press, 1974.

Morrill, W. H., Oetting, E. R., & Hurst, J. C. Dimensions of counselor functioning. *Personnel and Guidance Journal,* 1974, **52**(6), 355–359.

Murry, J. P. The comparative effectiveness of student-to-student and faculty advising programs. *Journal of College Student Personnel,* 1972, **13**(6), 562–566.

Pyle, R. R., & Snyder, F. A. Students as paraprofessional counselors at community colleges. *Journal of College Student Personnel,* 1971, **12**, 259–262.

Shook, H. R. Students on admissions committees: Should they vote on college applicants? *College Board Review,* 1970, **77**, 20–21.

Smith, D. Preferences of university students for counselors and counseling settings. *Journal of College Student Personnel,* 1974, **15**(1) 53–57.

Upcraft, M. L. Undergraduate students as academic advisors. *Personnel and Guidance Journal,* 1971, **49**, 827–831.

Walz, G. R. Innovations in student services. *Student Personnel Abstracts,* Winter 1971, 225.

Ware, C., & Gold, B. *Los Angeles City College peer counseling program.* Los Angeles: Los Angeles City College, 1970.

Ware, C. and Gold, B. The Los Angeles City College peer counseling program. Washington, D.C.: American Association of Junior Colleges, 1971.

Wolff, T. Undergraduates as campus mental health workers. *Personnel and Guidance Journal,* 1969, **48**, 294–304.

Zimpfer, D. G. (Ed.) Paraprofessionals in counseling, guidance, and personnel services. APGA Reprint Series No. 5. Washington, D.C.: APGA Press, 1973.

Zunker, V. G., & Brown, W. F. Comparative effectiveness of student and professional counselors. *Personnel and Guidance Journal,* 1966, **44,** 738–743.

Chapter 8

THE NEW STUDENTS AT THE CITY UNIVERSITY OF NEW YORK: HOW ARE THEY FARING?

Raymond Murphy

When the list of graduates from Brooklyn College (one of the three highest colleges in terms of academic standing in the City University of New York) arrived in the university's office of Paraprofessional Programs in June 1974, it included the names of 13 paraprofessionals: nine had received a B. A. and four, a B. S. Three names were followed by *summa cum laude;* two, by *cum laude.* The highest academic recognition that the city university offers had been given to five of the 13 graduates who were working as paraprofessionals in the city's public school system.

In the final report on a Title I umbrella program in a Brooklyn school district, reference was made to an optional-assignment remedial reading program at one junior high school and one intermediate school. Three regularly licensed teachers and one educational assistant were assigned to the program. "The educational assistant *who appeared to coordinate the program* seemed to be the most experienced of all [italics added]" and lacked only a few credits for graduation. Overall, the teachers in the program found that paraprofessionals were most helpful in small groups and with individual children (100 per cent in each), in keeping records (95 per cent), in preparing instructional materials (76 per cent), and in serving as a source of affection and comfort for the children (76 per cent). The paraprofessionals' responses confirmed these percentages. This seems to be generally true throughout the system. Where there are paraprofessionals, there is a warm, friendly atmosphere, even in makeshift classrooms; children are more comfortable, and teachers get more done because they have assistance in teaching as well as in routine duties.

These are only two stories about paraprofessionals: one from the colleges and the other from the schools where they work. However, they illustrate how well accepted paraprofessionals have become. The fact that many are able to take charge of a classroom or graduate from college with honors needs no comment.

BACKGROUND

Although the school aide and school volunteer program in New York City dates back many years, the participants were not viewed as professionals or even potential professionals. The school aide program, which began in 1957, was set up specifically to relieve teachers of nonteaching chores such as collecting milk money and escorting children. At first, the school volunteer program was a pilot project introduced by the Public Education Association with financial assistance from the Ford Foundation. Volunteers served in a variety of capacities, but especially pioneered in tutoring children with reading difficulties. This program too has now become permanent, and is an official unit under the jurisdiction of the Board of Education. The concepts of

saving teachers for teaching and providing individual tutoring for pupils were part of the background of the paraprofessional idea.

The paraprofessional program owes its existence primarily to the War on Poverty and the political climate of the
sixties. A number of ideas came together and seemed to be
fulfilled in the program. The slums were rediscovered and
renamed ghettos in common terminology and poverty-
impacted areas in federal legislation. Just as Sputnik had
shocked and challenged American education, now came
the discovery that the economically deprived children of
the ghettos were also educationally deprived—i.e., short-
changed on the traditional American means of rising toward equality. The obvious need for federal aid to
education, which had been balanced against the presumed
danger to local control (which then meant cities and states)
was given impetus by the personal interest of President
Johnson, a former school teacher. A series of legislative
enactments followed.

Head Start was the beginning. It signaled an interest
in early childhood education and a belief that by providing
poor children with an early start, food, a stimulating work
and play environment, the comforting presence of neighborhood residents in what was potentially an alien environment, the schools could compensate for many of the
difficulties these children faced. Head Start was rooted in
the community approach as part of the antipoverty effort.
A new group of auxiliary jobs supplemented teaching and
focused on liaison work with parents and the community
and their active participation in the program. These positions introduced into the classroom neighborhood residents, young and old, as assistants. (see chapter by Drije)

An equally important trend began with the Economic
Opportunity Act (EOA)—the basic Congressional enact-
ment of the War against Poverty—with its emphasis on jobs
and job training. The U.S. Department of Labor had, of

course, predecessor manpower programs, but they tended to aid the fittest (those most able to absorb training and to obtain jobs) rather than the neediest. EOA was designed to help people who were too poor to meet the criteria of traditional governmental programs.

Aid for entire neighborhoods and areas was made possible in the struggle against poverty. Thus more funds were available for community services, including not only the schools, but health, welfare, and legal agencies. A corollary to this was the idea that neighborhood people could be trained to supply these services, and as they obtained gainful employment, that too would be a boost for the entire community.

All these factors contributed to the concept that neighborhood residents could not only be given public service jobs to help them and their communities out of poverty, they could also learn on the job and through special education so that they began as paraprofessionals working with professionals and eventually become, through a planned career ladder, full-fledged professionals.

In the schools the emphasis was always on the children. Funds came primarily from the Elementary and Secondary Education Act of 1965, especially under Title I. The New York City Board of Education undertook a "strengthened early education program" rather than a paraprofessional program in 1968. Its purpose was to improve the quality of education in poverty-impacted areas, and one of its components involved using paraprofessionals in the classroom and training them for steadily greater contributions. During this period, there was a scarcity of teachers. It had already been recognized that if teachers were freed from noninstructional tasks, they would have more time to give personal attention to students and be innovative in the classroom. Poor student achievement and the large number of dropouts were also related to lack of communication and sometimes hostility and alienation among students, parents, and the community, on the one hand, and the compulsory government school and its educated and affluent personnel on the other. Differences in language as well as culture deepened the gap. Bringing neighborhood residents into the schools would bridge that gap.

The 1968 program was instituted by the New York City Board of Education in cooperation with the Manpower Career and Development Agency (MCDA) of the city's Human Resources Administration (HRA). MCDA's emphasis was on training and career development, and the agency agreed to pay the tuition of paraprofessionals who wished to continue their education. The Board of Education worked out a career ladder, and six community colleges in the city university system agreed to participate.

The only qualifications for entrance into the Paraprofessional Teacher Education Program (PTEP) were employment as an educational assistant in public primary schools and high school graduation or equivalency. (The board offered a high school equivalency program to those who were not high school graduates.) Most of the 858 original students who enrolled in PTEP in the spring of 1968 took English and speech courses. By fall a broader program in education and liberal arts was available. Students spent approximately six hours a week in classes and received about one day of released time from the job in return. MCDA not only covered the cost of college tuition and books, but provided stipends to defray the cost of incidentals and tutorial and counseling services.

Following the precedent set by Head Start, the Board of Education employed auxiliary personnel as teacher aides, family workers, educational assistants, and family assistants in elementary school classrooms in poverty areas and established the basis for a career ladder. The title of educational or family associate was given to those who finished the community college curriculum and earned Associate in Arts or Associate in Applied Science degrees.

These individuals were encouraged to transfer to the senior colleges to obtain the baccalaureate degree and then the teaching license. It was clear that there were at least two distinct career ladders (and the board suggested several others): one for teachers and one for social service or community workers.

As the War on Poverty was lost in the war on Vietnam and as national perspectives moved to the right under a business-oriented administration, the paraprofessional program in New York City received new impetus and stability. One unanswered question about the viability of the paraprofessional concept from the beginning was how professionals would react to these informal additions to their ranks. Would they view paraprofessionals as a threat to a status they had painfully won over the years? Perhaps paraprofessionals were acceptable in a time of great expansion of services and shortage of personnel in the sixties, but not in the cutback, job-security climate of the seventies.

THE TRADE UNION PROGRAM

What made the difference in New York was the attitude of trade unions that decided to attempt to organize paraprofessionals rather than treat them as competitors. As a result, the classroom paraprofessionals voted in 1969 to join the United Federation of Teachers while the family/community service workers voted to join Local 372, District Council 37, of the American Federation of State, County, and Municipal Employees. Each union agreement contains an article providing for career training. As a result of these contracts, the New York City Board of Education assumed financial responsibility for paraprofessional training at the college level. The first MCDA/HRA program ended in June 1972. At that time more than 2,000 paraprofessionals were studying at the city university, and six community colleges and eight senior colleges were also participating.

There have been two great advantages in obtaining the paraprofessional career programs through union contracts: first, they have become a permanent part of the school structure and, second, their financing is fixed, stable, and generous. Thus when similar programs in other parts of the country are hurt by economy drives and cutbacks, the New York program not only goes forward but the paraprofessionals' influence grows. For example, the following increases occurred in the PTEP budget between January 1, 1973, and December 31, 1974:

Semester	Amount
Spring 1973	$ 456,870
Summer 1973	400,000
Fall 1974	300,000
Total	$1,156,870

The two union contracts are specific and detailed about the benefits as well as training that the paraprofessionals are entitled to, and they are parallel. Three sections of the contracts deal with the paraprofessional education program. Funds for the program are among the benefits listed under provisions for the Welfare Fund. The section on rates of pay describes the rates as closely tied to achievement in the educational program. A separate contract article about career training outlines the programs for released time during the school year and for stipends to attend summer school.

In summary, the salary schedules for classroom paraprofessionals recognize no less than eight categories of paraprofessionals based on experience and education: Teacher Aide and Teacher Aide A; Educational Assistant and Educational Assistant A-I, A-II, and B; Educational Associate, and Auxiliary Trainer. The highest grade calls for 60 semester hours of approved college courses and three years of experience as an educational assistant, educational associate, or both; or 90 semester hours of approved college courses and two years of experience in the program. The pay differential between the starting and final categories is $2.22 an hour. Similarly, there are eight categories for home liaison personnel: Family Worker and Family Worker A; Family Assistant, Family Assistant A-I, A-II, and B; Family Associate, and Parent Program Assistant.

The career training section specifies that the Board of Education will make available each school year to all employees covered by the agreement (whether or not they are members of the union) six semester hours of career training each semester and six additional semester hours of career training during the summer. In the summer, the board will make available a six-week college-career training program (or a six-week high school equivalency program). During the school year, the paraprofessional receives released time of two to three hours each week, depending on the work week, or two hours pay if she works only 20 hours per week. A weekly stipend of $80 or $85 is paid to employees who work a 27½ or 30-hour week (but not to those who work fewer hours or are employed during the summer) for satisfactory attendance at summer school. This is part of the union's long-range program to ensure a full year's work for the paraprofessionals.

The Office of Paraprofessional Programs, City University of New York (CUNY), acts as a liaison among the other components of the program: the Board of Education, the Research Foundation (the university's fiscal agency), the unions, the 18 colleges of the university system that now participate, the school district and college coordinators, and the paraprofessionals themselves. Eight community colleges and ten senior colleges are currently participating in the program.

THE PARAPROFESSIONALS THEMSELVES

The paraprofessionals are neighborhood residents by definition; they live near the schools in which they teach and share the low-income status of their pupils. Most of them are women. Coming first from poverty-impacted areas (although the use of paraprofessionals has now spread throughout the system), they are preponderantly black and Puerto Rican, with numbers of Italians in some areas and a representative sprinkling of the ethnic mix of the entire city. (Two new related developments, greater attention to the handicapped and the use of paraprofessionals at the high school level, are beginning to change this picture, but slowly.)

Paraprofessionals tend to be between 35 and 45 years of age and have school-age grown children. In addition to working 20 to 30 hours a week in the classroom and managing a household, they are often active in community affairs (which is how they heard about their jobs). Thus it is surprising that they are able to fit college training into their busy schedules, and some dropouts and difficulties should be expected.

Between 3,000 and 4,000 (about one-fourth) of the paraprofessionals participate in PTEP, and the number who have, at one time or other, been involved may be considerably greater. The number enrolled in the city's community and senior colleges in the spring semester, 1974, was 3,589. One district threw considerable light on this by reporting that only about 50 of the 350 to 650 paraprofessionals in that district (minimum and maximum number employed) lacked college experience. Because of the irrational distribution of funds, it is often possible for districts to hire twice as many paraprofessionals in the second term and toward the end of the year as in the beginning. Thus those who were considered PTEP dropouts in the fall semester might simply have been waiting to be rehired and are unaware that they may be able to attend college in the interim. Illness, not necessarily of the paraprofessional herself, but of a child or a member of the family, may cause her to lose several weeks time. Because the effort required for that term seems insuperable she stays out altogether. A financial strain or crisis may make the extra expenditures impossible. Although not great, these expenditures are not negligible: Carfare adds up; there is no allowance for books, writing materials, and incidental essentials that some other programs include.

The important point to keep in mind is that although the college may complain about dropouts and the school about inconsistency and released time problems, the paraprofessional probably still considers herself part of the program—maybe she will not be in class this week or this month, but she is still fundamentally there. She sees a health or a financial problem; she does not see herself as a problem.

Considering the obstacles, the motivation of most paraprofessionals must be great and be based on more than tangible monetary rewards. At the rate of 18 credits a year (six each semester and summer school) it takes more than three years to obtain a two-year degree and twice as long to earn a bachelor's degree. Seven to ten years is a long time to hold three jobs (home, school, and college), jobs that do not end on the hour.

Paraprofessionals may have difficulty fitting into campus life—a life that is radically different from the ghetto neighborhood. They are not always placed in classes with other students; often they attend in the late afternoon or early evening, when others are not around. Because of their busy lives, they have little time for extracurricular activities. Yet they are not as different as the statistics imply. Most students are just out of high school, but evening classes have been a way of life for New Yorkers for decades. And older students, for whom the high schools and the private colleges have long provided services, are moving into the public colleges as well. For example, approximately 40 per cent of the 16,000 students that attend Queensborough Community College are over 21: 3,840 are between 22 and

29 years of age, 1,433 are in their thirties, 817 are in their forties, and 539 are 50 or older. The student of the future is apt to be in and out of school several times, employed, older, and preparing for some king of public service job. And he or she is more apt to be from a low-income minority group than before.

Sometimes paraprofessionals have specific reasons for not entering the program. In one Brooklyn district, all members of a group of paraprofessional librarians are a little above the average age level (35-45 years). They do not want full-time jobs; 20 hours a week seems about right. Although their incomes may make life a little easier, they do not support their families. The job itself is technical rather than stimulating. They are satisfied, so why should they take on more?

This is illustrative, but it does not explain why there are not more paraprofessionals in the program. Part of the answer lies in the districts. Some districts send a large proportion of their paraprofessionals to college, encouraging and following them every step of the way. Other districts send comparatively few, and it is not hard to understand that the lack of the initial encouragement to make the break, to step out of the neighborhood and away from the family, is a large part of the reason. But the end of the teacher shortage and the beginning of budget-tightening may motivate more paraprofessionals to undertake additional schooling as a means of protecting their jobs.

Although exact figures are lacking, between 400 and 500 paraprofessionals have probably earned the bachelor's degree, and more are coming. They coped, left their mark on the colleges and made it a little easier for the next group, and were influenced themselves. Take the basic matter of career, for instance. Employment in the schools gave neighborhood residents an opportunity, but it did not give them what more fortunate people have—a choice. They accepted the jobs they could find in the schools and went on from there with the presumed goal of teaching (even family workers were sometimes steered into teacher education because that was the main thrust of the program). But once in community college, vistas opened. Some thought of becoming secretaries in the business world; others considered social work or nursing; others learned audiovisual techniques that led to different worlds. None of these changes were overt. They were manifested in the form of murmurs and questions, of technical problems in one administrative office or other. Can I get credit for this course? What happens if I take this course instead of that?

The PTEP program can provide training for all these vocations and others because these vocations are also professions within the school system. That they offer opportunities outside the school system as well can be viewed as an infringement of the contract or as an advantage, especially in a time of decreasing opportunities in teaching. However, the fact that must be reckoned with is simple enough: paraprofessionals are making decisions for themselves. Opportunity is not enough. Choice is better.

CURRICULUM

Because almost all paraprofessionals begin their work in the community colleges, they are there by the hundreds and usually make up a full department (*the* teacher education department, although not often called that) and a full special "para" curriculum. The following sample curricula leading to the Educational Associate AA (or AAS) degree illustrate the typical broadly based program.

The senior colleges have no special department for paraprofessionals. Thus, these students become part of the general teacher education department and student body. The department has a coordinator and sometimes other personnel, financed by PTEP to keep track of them and provide counseling. But from the college catalogs, it is impossible to tell that the program exists; day sessions, full-time, and other exclusionary phrases are in evidence. Transfers from community college to senior college sometimes proceed smoothly and sometimes they do not. The range runs from total lack of communication to advance notice of which upcoming graduates wish to enroll. There is better understanding now than at the beginning about what credits can be transferred and what the requirements for senior college enrollment are, but the senior colleges make these decisions independently rather than on the basis of any cooperative agreement.

There is an inherent and basic conflict over curriculum between the community and the senior colleges, and paraprofessionals are caught in the middle. The community college has the student for a total of only two years (but often spread over three or four calendar years) and has no control over whether a student will receive further education. Thus the community college must stress vocational aspects, even while it tries to lay a broad educational foundation, for it must return the student to the job better equipped. The senior college, on the other hand, has a tradition of two years of generalized education followed by two years of specialization. Community college preparation suits neither situation, and the senior colleges have not been flexible enough to adapt to changing needs.

CUNY's structure is not helpful in relation to such problems—in fact it helped create them, for many of the colleges that make up CUNY are older than CUNY. Their admissions, curriculum, matriculation, and credit policies were formed when they were separate colleges. As a result, there are now 18 different sets of standards on a variety of

At one college	*At another*

English/humanities
  Composition
  Elective (language/culture)
	Fundamental composition
	  (core requirement)
	Fundamental communication
	  (core requirement)
	Humanities A (choice of English, communications, modern languages)

Math/Science
  Structure of the number
    system (2)
  Elective (natural environment)
	Survey of mathematics I (core requirement)
	Biology, chemistry, or physics
	Critial health issues (core requirement)

Social Science
  Introduction
	History of western civilization
	  (core requirement)
	Choice: one course in history or two courses in social science
	Humanities B
	  Choice: one course in music or art

Cooperative education
  Four internship seminars
	Education Associate Curricula
	  Behavioral Sciences Foundation of Education workshop I and II

academic topics. Paraprofessionals' problems are currently compounded by the fact that the senior colleges are preparing to change to a system of competency-based teacher education, which will imply new standards for transfer.

The home liaison paraprofessionals (family workers) have even greater problems. Only one college has a separate coordinator for community service workers and has worked out a degree program that is as clear and detailed as the program for teacher education. In fact, in 1974, in answer to requests, the program was opened to nonparaprofessional students as well. A list of the program's courses indicates the differences in emphasis between the two programs: Introduction to Social Service Agencies, followed by Current Trends in Social Service, and then Social

At one college	*At another*
Education Associate curricula	Reading and language arts for
General psychology	early childhood and elemen-
Urban sociology	tary years
Foundations of education	Elective (one of the follow-
Principles and practices of	ing):
early childhood	Contemporary urban educa-
Sociology of the family	tion
	School and community rela-
	tions in urban schools
	Introduction to learning
	problems
	Cooperative educational
	work experience
	Creative experiences for
	early childhood and elemen-
	tary years
Psychology	
Abnormal or social psychology	
or group dynamics	
Electives	
Liberal arts (12 credits)	Child Care Associate (an alter-
Unrestricted (6 credits)	nate program)
	Behavioral Sciences Founda-
	tion Education workshop I
	and II
	Day care seminar I and II
	Electives (16 or 17 credits)

Service Practicum and Seminar; Elements of Sociology, Urban Sociology, Social Aspects of Poverty; Introduction to Psychology, Group Dynamics; English composition, Spanish, liberal arts, and science electives.

Most of the other colleges now have curricula called human services, public service or something similar, and there is some direct preparation for a social service work career. The problem lies in transferring a paraprofessional student who is technically classified as PTEP into another department through a maze of parochialism.

THE INSTITUTIONS

Original Perspectives.

PTEP's planners expected the colleges to be more flexible than they actually were. Planning was done by representatives of the Board of Education; HRA (which made the greatest programmatic contribution), and CUNY. In response to the initial suggestions of the planners, the board set up the Auxiliary Educational Career Unit in its Office of Personnel. This unit worked out the basics of the program: e.g., which schools should be covered and how many auxiliaries could be afforded; orientation and preservice and in-service training for them; and the career ladder. As an apparent compromise, the first choice of auxiliaries was on a 50-50 basis, an equal number of opportunities for people already working in the schools and for nominees of the Community Progress Corporations or other local antipoverty agencies.

> The career ladder approach represents an alternative method leading to a professional degree. It is essential that new types of experiences become part of this effort. [In other words, CUNY was asked] . . . to have "work and life experiences" as an accepted part of an A.A. degree, with college credits assigned to these experiences;
>
> the expansion of high school equivalency and skills training program to provide for 3,400 students by September 1967 (to make possible participation in this program of increased numbers of participants from the Neighborhood Youth Corps and Scheuer programs);
>
> to have representatives of HRA-MCDA, the Board, and the community appointed as participating members of the curriculum coordinating committee established by the City University to plan the new program;
>
> to offer programs and courses off campus;
>
> to credit courses taken by students in September 1967 (before the program was fully developed) toward the A.A. Supportive tutorial assistance was listed but responsibility for it had not yet been determined.

Perhaps the key statement was

> It is essential that the cooperating agencies be part of the on-going planning process. In addition, the community representatives may make suggestions that would be helpful in accommodating the special needs of participants indigenous to that community. It is important to set up a mechanism for keeping this central coordinating committee appraised of all of the decisions made by the faculty curriculum planning committee in each community college.

The representative planning and participation outlined in the memo was never established. While the program went ahead on the local school level, the strong impetus for community participation provided by the federal government met with opposition. In New York City the forces concerned with educational opportunities for the poor were directing their attention toward the achievement of open enrollment at the university. Because open enrollment made the greater demands for innovative programming in the colleges, it met with greater resistance. The rather small paraprofessional component (which did not begin to reach the senior colleges until the seventies) suffered benign neglect.

Programmatic Vacuum

No single entity has been assigned the responsibility for thinking and acting programmatically about the program. Technically, it is well taken care of, except for problems connected with transfer credits and the like on an individual basis. But with the disappearance of HRA and the coming of the union, with its concentration on traditional union benefits and grievances, there is no overall view. Occasionally, when a major issue such as credit for "practice teaching" in the schools becomes urgent, policy must be thrashed out. In this case it was done on the state level, but even when standards for acceptance of paraprofessional work in the schools became legally effective, the senior colleges retained their separate control.

The Board, the Union, and the Colleges

The Bureau of Pre-Service Training functions in terms of carrying out its responsibilities under provisions of the union contracts—and finds that whenever a point is disputed, its administrative superior, the Office of Personnel, which has no experience in the program, takes charge. The colleges pretend that the paraprofessionals do not exist, that they are students like any other students; in other words, any adjusting to be done will be done by the paraprofessionals. For the college, it amounts to a bit more paperwork, which brings additional added funds and kudos.

The summer session problem illustrates conflicting viewpoints. The union views the summer-school stipend as part of the approach to ensuring year-round employment for the paraprofessionals. For this reason, as well as the problem of conflicting class schedules, it wants a summer school that begins after the public school term ends (which in 1975 was June 30th). The board, understanding the reasoning and bound by the contract to offer six weeks of summer school, has successfully implemented this proposal, but not without a continuous struggle with some colleges.[1] They protest the dates, the rise in the number of paraprofessionals enrolled during the summer, and the fact (decided in arbitration) that paraprofessionals need take only one or more, not six credits to qualify for the stipend. Many paraprofessionals attend summer school, partially because they need the income, but perhaps equally because those who are unable to undertake the additional burden of college while working can do so as an alternative to work in the summer.

It is natural for groups to have conflicting interests and differ on any number of things. What seems odd and unfortunate is that the colleges refuse to treat the paraprofessionals who only attend summer sessions as serious students. They view the situation as a problem for the education departments rather than as an opportunity to reach and influence individuals who are not normally exposed to ideas and training on the college level. If the colleges thought programmatically about these students, for instance, by this time one of them might have come up with a special teacher-training institute, held only in the summer, with a course planned over several years for what they call "perennials."[2] The identity problem of the family workers that was discussed earlier is another aspect of nonthinking about paraprofessionals.

PARAPROFESSIONALS AT WORK

Paraprofessionals are somewhat restricted by state legislation and administrative rulings, but not much. They must work under the supervision of a professional, and they may not assume responsibility for an entire class. Complaints are still sometimes heard from paraprofessionals who are allowed to do only routine work such as putting equipment away, helping children with their coats, keeping records, and so forth. This usually occurs in districts and schools where paraprofessionals are new. These are also apt to be places where a paraprofessional must bring a grievance to obtain released time, and if college is accepted, it is not encouraged. The trouble is not so much the dispute and its resolution as the fact that only a highly unusual paraprofessional (one who is not yet in the program and who has outside experience, status, and assistance) will insist on her rights—or indeed, be aware of them—in an unfriendly environment. It is another reason why most paraprofessionals

are not in PTEP. A summary of what most paraprofessionals do in the classroom includes the following duties: participating in planning, working with small groups, working
with individual pupils, serving as a source of affection and
comfort to children, keeping records, preparing instructional materials.[3] In a good school situation, paraprofessionals participate increasingly in teaching the children,
and their role expands from that of neighborhood friend to
that of skilled professional as their education nears completion.

The activities cited were, of course, those of classroom
paraprofessionals. The breakdown of responsibilities carried out in one school year by two family assistants assigned
to a special reading program was as follows: eight contacts
with outside agencies, 42 home visits, 238 contacts with
parents, including telephone calls, 38 children tutored and
served on a regular basis, 23 parent workshops attended,
55 reading center staff training sessions attended, and 57
conferences with center staff about individual children.

Try to envision a situation where one teacher must
function as the liaison between the school and her pupils'
families. How many of the 238 telephone calls could have
taken place, especially if some of the parents spoke only
Spanish, Italian, or Chinese?

LOOKING FORWARD

The future of the paraprofessionals should be assured. But
although it may be for the group, what about the individual?

Paraprofessionals are accepted, even institutionalized,
in the schools. The idea of qualified helpers for teachers—
team teaching and other innovations at a budget price—
will not disappear. (But the paraprofessional might if, under the impact of competency-based teacher education,

schools turn to students sent from teacher education departments rather than to neighborhood residents. The union will offer some defense against this, but the primary defense, in the community organizations that furnish the people, is weak now.) Perhaps career-ladder paraprofessionals are also threatened by the tight job market, which includes but is not limited to education. More and more individuals with bachelor's degrees, including teachers, who cannot find jobs for which they are qualified, are applying for jobs as paraprofessionals. This will mean more pressure on the paraprofessionals to complete their education. But it may also mean fewer jobs for neighborhood paraprofessionals. So many factors, including not only the economy but the disposition of local boards and supervisory personnel, are involved that predictions are hazardous.

The position of the family workers is less secure and more dependent on union pressure. They are not accepted as essential as teachers are. Their funding rests more and more on city sources alone and the city budget is in bad shape. Some family workers have transferred or have tried to transfer to classroom positions, despite the surplus of applicants there. Yet if family workers can hold their jobs long enough to complete their education—and in their own field, not in that of the teachers—their opportunities may well be better because of the expansion and increasing complexity of human services.

Here are some hard facts. The United Federation of Teachers placed an advertisment in the *New York Times* in the spring of May 1974 to boast, justifiably, about paraprofessionals. But one of the things the ad said was that 300 had graduated from the colleges and 100 of these graduates were employed in the schools. This is nothing to boast about! With a turnover of 7,000 to 8,000 paraprofessionals in the school system each year, why couldn't 200 be placed, despite the lack of expansion in the teaching staff? Did some of them graduate without the proper courses or credits? This has happened, and the colleges cannot simply refuse to assume responsibility for it. Did these graduates fail the National Teacher Examination (NTE)? Some did, but how many, and out of how many? And again, why? Were they only eligible for employment (as the NTE-only people are) in low reading-achievement schools that could not employ them because of cutbacks? Or did some districts or schools simply give preference to nonparaprofessionals?

True, many paraprofessionals have become successful teachers, and they have proved that the career ladder works. But the employment of one-third of them is not a passing grade, and somebody owes it to the other two-thirds to find out why. Again the hiatus between program and policy is evident.

The gloomy side of the picture should not deter would-be paraprofessionals from trying to become paraprofessionals or to embark on the long road to the baccalaureate. There ought to be a bright side to the picture, and they as citizens can help create it. First, there should not be fewer teachers in the schools; that is poor economy. Smaller classes, help for the handicapped, specialized services—our pupils need all the help they can get, and that means *more* and *better* teachers. Second, community residents belong in the schools, and on all levels, and having gained a foothold, they should not yield it to the economy or anything else. Third, regardless of setbacks, day care is a coming field, whether seen from the viewpoint of working parents or the philosophy of early childhood development. Trained teachers and family workers can make day care more than custodial.

Finally, as paraprofessionals in PTEP are finding out for themselves, education opens many doors and vistas, not just the door to the classroom from which they come. If the Board of Education and the unions, the major determinants of policy, could take this broad view of the para-professionals' future (because of the economic slowdown, they may be less reluctant to) then the program could be even more helpful to paraprofessionals. And the "multiplier effect" would aid communities that need more of an economic boost now than they did in the optimistic sixties.

NOTES

1. Apparently, the colleges fail to understand the nature of a program derived from collective bargaining, which includes an adversary relationship between the board and the union and binding responsibilities that third parties cannot alter.

2. Summer school has been viewed since its origin as a place where teachers can obtain special training that is not available in their localities during the school year. The idea is not new or startling nor is it necessarily the answer. It would, however, demonstrate that someone is trying to think about helping paraprofessionals on their own terms.

3. This list of duties was obtained from a questionnaire distributed to teachers in one district who worked with paraprofessionals in a remedial reading program.

Editors note: As part of the cutbacks at both the City University and the Board of Education during the summer of 1976, the Paraprofessional Teacher Education Program was discontinued. It is both a comment about the extent of the paraprofessionals interest in education and a tribute to their seriousness that, nonetheless, most of them continued as enrolled students at the colleges, but now without tuition support from the Board of Education or special services from the colleges.

Chapter 9

THE CAREER OPPORTUNITIES PROGRAM: A SUMMING UP

W. Thomas Carter

Objectives and Means

From its inception in 1969 as the largest new program originating from the authority of the Education Professions Development Act (EPDA) of June 1967, the Career Opportunities Program (COP) was conceived as a means for addressing such central educational issues as:

strengthening the self and group identity of the children of the poor, the minorities, and the alienated;

using training programs as an instrument of and catalyst for educational change;

bringing new and different persons into the schools to play new and different roles; and

developing relations of equality (parity) among participants, school, communities being served, and colleges.

The centerpiece of COP was the paraprofessional teacher aide, who was usually a minority (54 percent Black,

14.3 percent Hispanic-American, 3.7 percent Native American) female (88 percent) and came from the neighborhood in which (s)he worked. This COP participant was destined, through COP, to receive college-based training which would qualify her/him for a teaching certificate as an ultimate objective and, in any case, improved performance and credentials as an aide. The total cost for the seven-year COP effort, of which five years represented local project activity, was approximately $130,000,000. The program embraced 132 sites, roughly 18,000 participants, close to 3,000 schools, and 272 colleges and universities.

While the Education Professions Development Act provided for a variety of specific activities, it also provided far-reaching and broad general authority, notably in Part D, for the establishment of new programs. The Career Opportunities Program, formally launched in 1970, is a product of that broad authority, for there is no mention of it—or of any program like it—in the language of the Education Professions Development Act. In that sense, it was the product of the Office of Education rather than of explicitly expressed Congressional intent.

A number of factors provided background to and impetus for the establishment of the Career Opportunities Program. Among these were:

> the perception in the middle and late 1960s of a present (and growing) teacher shortage, especially in and for schools serving the poor;
>
> the recognition that the educational needs of low-income children were not being met by the schools as then staffed;
>
> the broader sense of the inadequacy of the ways schools in general were staffed;
>
> the positive experience of the early 1960s with the employment of community-based paraprofessionals, particularly in the anti-poverty program but also in schools; and
>
> the growing belief that the then-present designs of teacher education were inadequate, particularly in preparing teachers for the children of the poor.

A new organizational entity, the Bureau of Educational Personnel Development (BEPD), was established to implement various of the programs established by the new EPDA. From the outset of both the legislation and BEPD, the principle new program was to be COP.

The COP design was relatively uncomplicated. It was to be a program of the U. S. Office of Education, which made grants to local school systems with the concurrence of the respective state departments of education to provide on-the-job training and college education to paraprofessionals working in schools serving low-income children. The participants would thereby mount a career ladder, earn a baccalaureate degree, and become eligible for a teacher's license. The training was provided in the schools by cooperating teachers, supervisory personnel, and Career Opportunities Program project staff, while the formal education was provided by a local college or university through a subcontract from the local COP project. With increased experience, training, and education, participants were expected both to become better teacher aides and, in most cases, to assume greater responsibility and status in the school system. At the end of the program and with a degree and a teacher's license having been earned, a process that usually took four to six years for a person beginning with no previous college experience, the participant was available for employment as a full-fledged teacher.

Although COP clearly was not meant to threaten the institutions with which it worked, the U. S. Office of Education did consider it to be one of several contributors to educational change across a broad front including access to higher education, the professional preparation of teachers, the increased involvement of the community in school matters, and the development of more complex staffing patterns for schools. Some COP projects weighed in significantly in all of these areas, while others had more impact in one or two. No COP project, it appears safe to say, failed to make some impression—at the least on the lives of the participants, at most on the futures of all of the institutions involved.

On access to higher education, the Career Opportunities Program was part of a broad array of forces pushing to break the near-monopoly of the young, white, middle- and upper-class full-time student. The Career Opportunities Program was unique in bringing to the colleges large numbers of students who were older and also workers.

Similarly, the Career Opportunities Program was only one of the forces working for changes in teacher education which would make it field-based, more inductive in curricula design, and more heavily focused upon demonstrable classroom competency. The special character of COP derived from the fullness of the field base, for the COP participants in the colleges' teacher education programs were simultaneously full-time classroom workers.

Not only were the Career Opportunities Program participants both workers in the school and students at the local college or university, they were also members of the community served by the school. Thus, the efforts of the Career Opportunities Program to develop increased community involvement in the school was not alone the work of a lay council seeking to play a governance role. By the presence of the participants, community involvement was by definition a central feature of each Career Opportunities Program project.

The employment of paraprofessionals in schools had preceded the Career Opportunities Program, and, during its existence, extended far beyond it; during the early 1970s the Career Opportunities Program participants accounted for fewer than five percent of the paraprofessionals in all schools. What was unique about the Career Opportunities Program in this regard was the fact that from their entry into the Career Opportunities Program, participants were engaged in activities directly related to pupil learning (and not shunted off to clerical or monitoring roles), and that the

COP design was not a static staff differentiation model. Rather, individual participants were involved in a career development design moving from entry-level paraprofessional positions to licensed teachers. And as the Career Opportunities Program emphasized the utilization of paraprofessionals in roles of substantial involvement in the teaching/learning process, it, of necessity (as well as plan), affected the activities of the teachers in the classrooms. And the net results of both these sets of activities was increased individualization of instruction for children.

COP was designed to serve low-income and minority adults. Nearly nine-tenths of those enrolled were members of low-income families, and some seven-tenths were non-white. The continuing shortage of teachers with such backgrounds is seen, for example, in Alaska where 95 percent of the children in the State Operated Schools are Native (Aleut, Eskimo, or Indian), while 99 percent of the teachers at the start of the COP project were non-Native. On the Crow and Northern Cheyenne Reservations in Montana, only five of the 210 certified teachers in 1970 were Indians. At their conclusion, the Alaska Career Opportunities Program (run in concert with the Teacher Corps) will have quintupled the number of Native teachers, while the project serving the Crow and Northern Cheyenne will have increased the number of Indian teachers tenfold.

Throughout the Hispanic-American and Indian communities there was still a woeful underrepresentation of "indigenous" teachers. In Texas and the Southwest, for example, COP projects emphasized bilingual and bicultural (Hispanic) education, and in New York City, a significant focus was placed in meeting the needs of part of that city's Puerto Rican children.

THE COP PARAPROFESSIONAL

The COP Project Directors Handbook described potential COP participants as "individuals who have the ability and desire to spend a significant part of their working careers in providing better education for children of low-income families," as residents of the area served by the COP schools, and as persons of "low-income background." These qualifications were met with only limited exceptions and deviations. Left unstated in the Handbook was the implicit understanding that "low-income" in many instances also meant "minority" and that the goals of the program were thus social and economic as well as educational.

Reporting on Pennsylvania's four COP projects (Smethport, Philadelphia, Scranton and Erie) in November 1974, a private evaluation firm, Educational Research Associates, noted the following:

> One of the specific objectives of this program was to introduce a different kind of person to the teaching field. This was interpreted to mean a kind of person who normally would not have gone to college to pursue a teacher preparation program. Consequently, these four projects involved, for the most part, people who normally would have been rejected in a standard admissions review.
>
> How did these different people make out in the academic game? One indication of their success is an almost incredibly low mortality rate; less than four per cent of all the COP participants were dropped from the program for academic problems. Yet another indication is provided by the project in Philadelphia which indicated in a survey of its participants that 85 percent had a C average or better and that 46 percent of the participants had an average of B or higher.
>
> Furthermore, in each project there are stories of the academic honors being bestowed on these "different" people. In each project there are participants who are on the Dean's List; in one project two of the COP participants are engaged in a very competitive race for the top average which is now in the neighborhood of 3.83 on a 4.0 scale. One specific indication of the academic honors already bestowed on these participants is that a total of 67 trainees have already graduated from college with honors.
>
> In the Philadelphia project alone, 27 students have already graduated with a grade point average of 3.5 or higher and

have been named Presidential Scholars. This is especially remarkable when one considers that these are people who normally would not have been admitted to the institution of higher education. There have been other achievements by these COP participants in their educational pursuits. In one of the projects a number of the students have been appointed or elected to leadership positions in the regular student body; one of them even being named to a national council. In the other projects these different students have participated in the drama, in the school newspaper, and in other activities of the school.

The centerpiece of any COP enterprise was the trainee —whether labeled aide, auxiliary (in New York City), paraprofessional, or intern (Vermont)—around whom all COP activities revolved. The story of COP was thus the story of the human beings who were in it, and on their success hinged COP's success. For the participant was the agent whose work determined fulfillment or failure across the entire range.

Near the midway point in COP's history, a national survey revealed that 13,477 persons had participated in the program and 9,343 were then enrolled as full-fledged trainees. Over 86 percent were low-income family heads or members, 63 percent were recruited from various other governmental programs, and 13 percent (this figure dwindled thereafter) were veterans of Vietnam-era military service. More than three-fourths of the trainees were non-white (54 percent Black, 14.3 Hispanic, 3.7 Native American, remainder scattered among Asian and others). Although the average participant was probably 31 or 32, COP also included teenagers and grandparents well into their sixties.

The people who became COP participants brought unique qualities and qualifications. The common personal denominators were a commitment to improving the educational performance of poor and/or minority children, the capacity to change careers, personal drive and ambition, and boundless stamina. Above all, her (or his) well developed sense of the needs of minority children was propelling her (or him) into the schools and beyond, into the postsecondary education that had never before been possible. With a few adjustments on both sides, such a person was a future teacher. Moreover, at a time when involvement in community affairs had become recognized as an indispensible feature of a good teacher training program, the COP participant *was* the community—from it, devoted to it, and determined to improve it. But release time was hard to come by, and COP people were often forced to lead three distinct lives—fulltime work in the schools, a crushing academic load, and, because most were mothers, the domestic life that seems inevitably to be the first to be neglected. The baby-sitting husband or wife was no rarity in the COP scheme of things.

The full weight of this set of forces sat too heavily on some. Without sufficient dedication and dexterity, pure logistics could make COP participation all but impossible, and as many as one-third of those who began lasted less than one year. But those who stayed were the embodiment of the nation's best qualities.

Illustrations of the qualities of COP's participants are the best demonstration of the enormous diversity of background and interests they possessed. Some random examples:

> A high school dropout employed as a janitor at Winston Elementary School in the Edgewood District of San Antonio, Texas, became a COP aide and enrolled at St. Mary's University
>
> The cumulative grade point average of the Saginaw, Michigan, aides was significantly higher than that of the student bodies of Delta and Saginaw Valley College as a whole
>
> Twenty-seven per cent of the participants in the Little Rock, Arkansas, project graduated with honors
>
> COP participants, according to a survey of the California COP effort "could often bring a welcome dose of their real

world experience to cloistered educational courses taught
by faculty who sometimes had not been in an elementary
school classroom for years."

Roberta Ellis of COP Minneapolis, in her mid-forties, a divorced mother, was a country club kitchen worker from 5
p.m. to 6 a.m., took care of six to seven children plus several
of her own in her home during the day, and somehow found
time to teach Sunday school. Determined to become a
teacher, she entered the Minneapolis New Careers program
as a school aide and assumed a 19-21 credit quarterly load
at the University of Minnesota. In August 1972, with five
months of hospitalization from an automobile accident behind her, she graduated from the university and became a
regular fifth grade teacher. Shortly thereafter, Ms. Ellis enrolled as a candidate for a graduate degree, one of countless
COP graduates who kept on learning long after their COP
phase had ended.

The average COP participant in the Gary, Indiana, COP
project had been away from formal education for 25 years.
And yet, in one year (1971-72), 43 COP aides were invited
to join a national academic sorority. Since then, 60 Gary
COP participants qualified for the Dean's List at the Purdue
University Calumet Campus.

Prior to his participation in COP, Eugene Witlock, a veteran
in the Louisville COP project, had been denied admission to
a state college. As part of COP, he graduated from the
University of Louisville while on the Dean's List and went on
as a district employee to co-author a proposal for the evaluation of COP and alone designed a paraprofessional training
institute in special education.

Not knowing it was improper, Gloria Enoex combined her
attendance at one college as part of COP with simultaneous
attendance in another, all this while working as a paraprofessional in the Grand Rapids, Michigan, schools. Having thus
earned her BA in two-and-a-half years, Ms. Enoex, a mother
of eight, went on to gain an MA as a reading specialist in six
months. One of Ms. Enoex's tactics, enabling her to do her
school work and keep up with her family, was to have one
of the children read to her as she cooked dinner.

Danny Gurule organized the recording of a disc featuring
New Mexico's Lieutenant Governor and Gurule's students

at Cristo Rey School in Santa Fe. The recording was done to raise money for a new school bus. Gurule completed his work at Santa Fe College and, unlike his fellow COP participants who will teach in the city's schools, he will become the Assistant Director of the College's Bilingual/Bicultural Studies Program. Already recognized with a listing in "Who's Who in American Colleges and Universities," Gurule is arranging with a publisher for use of bilingual materials he developed while in COP.

Participants in the Miami, Florida, COP project formed a COP alumni association which, among other goals pledged that it would form a scholarship fund for participants who had not graduated by the scheduled termination of the project. The Racine, Wisconsin, COP alumni group also organized and declared itself to be an available source to the Racine school district.

Of 25 COP Richmond trainees attending Contra Costa College in California in the 1971-72 school year, 16 made the Dean's List. Three more received additional academic honors. Preliminary data indicate that in the larger COP world, the COP trainee was a better student than his or her non-COP peers—all this, of course, while holding an aide's job and running a family.

Mrs. Ruth Winney, a Navajo Indian in her fifties, began her formal education as a seven-year-old at a boarding school in Fort Defiance, Arizona, spent the rest of her childhood and early youth in schools away from home, and with a high school diploma to her credit, became an assistant in a Bureau of Indian Affairs School. The job could lead nowhere. College credits were unavailable, and the closest college was over 200 miles away. Then came the new Navajo Community College and COP, and Mrs. Winney was on her way.

In Baltimore, Maryland, 93 percent of the COP graduates held teaching posts in the city system by September 1975.

From the age of nine, Richard Gatica of Crystal City, Texas, spent at least half of every year as a migrant worker in the North. He left school after the eighth grade. In the Army, Gatica received a high school equivalency degree (GED) and, after discharge, held several jobs while amassing two years of postsecondary credits. An outstanding student in his COP years at Southwest Texas Junior College in Uvalde and Texas A&I in Laredo, he graduated early and assumed a bilingual teaching post in 1972. In 1974 Gatica was selected to be director of the same COP program which had given him his professional start.

These were almost random selections. In an era replete with inspirational tales of tardily discovered human potential unleashed, it became axiomatic that COP's dominant strength would be found in the aides. For every "ordinary" COP striver, there was a Dallas mother of eight who maintained a 4.0 grade average or an Indian COP graduate appointed to a presidential advisory council or a disabled Black Vietnam veteran giving hope to ghetto children in New Orleans. It was thoroughly predictable that such people, more even than their communities or institutions or COP staff, would give the COP sites their real character. And they were never in short supply.

THE EFFECTS OF COP ON THE SCHOOLS

Images of COP in the schools are as varied as images of the 132 separate COP projects. In a few school systems COP was probably little more than a wispy, federally-funded program; in many others, it provided the impetus for important change along broad lines, with no single factor, but rather an amalgam of forces, emerging as the central COP contribution. COP was not just a popular front organization charged with advising or even sharing decision-making authority with the public school hierarchy. Nor was it just the physical presence of a COP aide in a Detroit or Navajo reservation classroom. The binding element was training. Closely linked was cultural and group identity. And for these, no amount of structural innovation—however valuable to the COP process were open classrooms, modular instruction, role differentiation, or any other—could provide an adequate substitute. As long as the basic conditions were met, the COP formula was flexible, with weighting of the mix left largely to the sensitive discretion of site administration.

> Training of COP aides represented a thoughtful blend of intellectual experiences and practical applications.
>
> Whether or not they had previously done it, teacher training institutions came to the community with site-based courses, on-site observation, and active participation in advisory councils—all adding up to an attempt by higher education to become part of a rapidly changing scene rather than an observer, advisor, or chronicler.
>
> The place of the educational paraprofessional in the schools was sanctioned and legitimatized through carefully constructed opportunities for rewarding careers, satisfying work, and the possibility of achieving higher professional status.
>
> Children in the COP schools were taught, more by example than from books, that being American Indian or Chicano or Puerto Rican or Cajun or Oriental or Black or hill country white was a source of pride and that these cultures should be nourished, not suppressed or discarded.

These were some of the main messages COP left in some school systems. Some of the concrete results stem from the messages, while others are nearly independent of them. Some outcomes, like those described below, were direct results of the availability and ability of the paraprofessionals and of the Career Opportunities Program.

> In Honolulu, 19 COP participants worked as teacher assistants at Honolulu Community College. They worked in the reading and audio-visual laboratories, at the computer science center, in the chemistry and biology laboratories, in student services, and in the art, electronics, and industrial arts departments. These were not, of course, "normal" sites for paraprofessional activity.
>
> In Minneapolis, COP participants managed an Indian Student Aide Program, while in Detroit, COP participants conducted a Youth Tutoring Youth Project involving 70 tutors and 280 tutees.

In Las Cruces, New Mexico, new relationships developed between school and community, largely through COP and through inter-institutional linkages in which COP played a prominent role.

At the start of the COP project in Jacksonville, Florida, the district employed 140 teacher aides. By 1974, there were 654, half supported by local funds. The example of the performance by the COP aides was a significant factor in the increase. At the initiation of COP, only the COP aides were on the career lattice; all 654 aides later joined.

As a result of the COP model, all paraprofessionals employed in the Trenton (N.J.) schools have improved salary schedules, pensions, sick leave, health insurance, and a career lattice—a process which became the standard in most of the school systems in which COP functioned.

Based upon the successful experience with COP, a district-wide School Development Center for all levels of personnel was established in Lewiston, Maine, by the school district, the University of Maine, and the state department of education. This innovation survived the end of funding.

School system renewal was heavily abetted in Peoria, Illinois, as a result of COP's co training of teachers and paraprofessionals.

In Pawtucket, Rhode Island, the COP project was found to be positive, conducive to better school operations, and "a credit" to all concerned.

Workships in humanizing education, career education, competency-based teacher education, among other topics, involved hundreds of Dade County (Fla.) teachers along with the COP participants.

In Cleveland, as part of the process of developing a performance-based evaluation of participants' student teaching experience, 60 teachers and principals participated in a semester-long series of intensive training workshops designed to build teacher competencies in supervisory, managerial, and minority responsibilities, and principal competencies in playing a professional leadership role in staff development.

Based upon the COP experience, the Rochester (N.Y.) school system used local funds to "buy" a college faculty position for teacher training.

In San Juan, Utah, COP project, LEA staff were used as field faculty by the IHE for on-site courses. The result was the improvement of LEA staff professional competency.

The inclusion of community people in a "needs assessment" in the design and ongoing revision of the Camden (N.J.) COP project has brought closer school-community collaboration. So, too, did the training of lay community people, a bilingual news report system, the community council, as well as, of course, the recruitment of COP participants from the community. In Camden, too, the integration of training programs for all 900 staff members (paraprofessionals, teachers, supervisors, and administrators) resulted from the COP initiative.

In addition to program activities, the Alaska COP projects provided services to children and the community, which included a preschool in Nondalton, a photography course in Togiak, a sports program in Tanana, a library in Nulato, translators in Bethel, ABE classes in Noorvik and Angoon, health services in Fort Yukon, and a Youth Tutoring Youth Program in Metlakatla.

At McKinleyville (California) High School, the Humboldt State University COP project discovered that 100, rather than the expected handful of Indian students were enrolled. Perceiving that many were actual or potential dropouts, the project conceived and instituted the Indian Students Retention Program.

The creation of career lattices, an important COP objective, in the five cooperating school districts of the Bay Area Bilingual Education League (BABEL) COP project in California meant that paraprofessionals would receive training in bilingual (Spanish, Chinese, or Philipino) education, a policy that greatly facilitated the addition of bilingual classes to school curricula.

Analyzing the impact of COP's four Pennsylvania projects (Smethport, Scranton, Erie, Philadelphia) on local school systems, the independent Educational Research Associates of Bowie, Maryland, judged that "the schools were affected in a positive way." The specific efforts were:

the greatly increased use of teacher aides,

a significant change in the way they were used,

the beneficial impact of aides on the environment (specifically, in the case of Erie with a history of racial tension and violence, the reduction and ultimate disappearance of the disturbances that had plagued one location),

an increased leadership role for teachers,

increased opportunities for minority administrators,

growing dependence on local neighborhoods as a source of new teachers, and

a general acknowledgment that the COP-trained teachers would be more effective than others who had entered the various systems.

To these benefits, a report from the Texas Education Agency adds the significant point that the COP projects in that state (Edinburg, Crystal City, El Paso, Fort Worth/Dallas, Houston, Milland, San Angelo, and Edgewood-San Antonio) had yielded increased community involvement. One measure of this was the practice of home visits by teachers and COP participants which, the report concluded, "resulted in better communication between parents, teachers, students, and school administrators." The report added, "the turnover rate of Career Opportunities Program aides has been very low, resulting in more stabilized and continuous community and parental involvement."

Many of the possible effects of COP on the schools cannot be attributed solely to this program. One, however, is an almost uniquely COP-generated force: the impact of paraprofessionals. Assessing this impact on the schools of Minneapolis and Duluth, Minnesota, the Minnesota Department of Education reported, "Teachers, school social workers, and principals spontaneously and repeatedly volunteered observations of:

the positive impact of COP aides upon the individualization of instructors, (and)

the importance of COP aides as a resource to the professional staff."

THE COLLEGES AND COP

For many of the 272 institutions of higher education involved in the program, the arrival of the Career Opportunities Program signaled important, often unanticipated, changes in the ways teachers were to be trained, students admitted, and instructional content delivered.

Although always central to the overall national COP design, the colleges and universities came, too, to occupy roles that had perhaps not been fully anticipated. Some of them, for example, became, willingly or not, the rough equivalents of remedial adult education centers. Many were introduced into new and different communities. A large majority adopted open admissions, at least for COP and COP-type applicants (older, more experienced, but perhaps initially less attuned to academe than their "regular" peers in the colleges). Most found themselves offering instruction in ghetto, barrio and/or Indian reservation public schools. And many who had hardly expected it found themselves adopting major shifts in the way they would train teachers—changes in practice teaching, more on-scene experience, increased emphasis on individualization, development of field-based practice, fewer theoretical and more practical situations and, possibly most important, institutional recognition that the post-secondary institution did not have all of the answers.

In fact, the mechanics of the COP arrangement, which featured the college as a sub-contractor of the school system, may have been one of COP's several most important contributions to teacher training in years to come. This was a role that must have required inordinately jarring adjustments for the larger, more established teacher training colleges and universities in the COP network. It could hardly have been easy for major state universities to make the necessary changes. And yet, before COP concluded, it had involved the state universities of Florida, Nebraska, Maine,

Massachusetts, Minnesota, New Hampshire, New Mexico, North Dakota, South Dakota, Vermont, Virginia, Wyoming and Washington—plus other public institutions too numerous to list. And private (or semi-public) colleges such as Boston University, The University of Southern California, Pittsburgh, Fordham, Temple, Mills and Texas Christian, also provided instruction to COP participants—with spillover effects that will be measurable only with the passage of time.

Some typical examples of what went on in COP's 272 colleges and universities (211 four-year and 61 two-year) demonstrate the range of experiences and accomplishments, many of them "firsts," of several of those institutions during and as a direct consequence of COP:

> The Idaho colleges involved in COP gave practicum credit, assisted in developing career lattices, and instituted some competency-based programs.
>
> At the 10,000-student University of Louisville, COP's 125 participants forced the adoption of an almost open admissions policy which credits maturity, personal background, and work experience. Even non-high school graduates may be provisionally accepted and given a trial semester in which to achieve unconditional admission.
>
> Brigham Young University in Utah did these things:
> 1. relaxation of admissions criteria for COP trainees and, when occasion demands, presumably for similar others,
> 2. introduction of Indian history and linguistics, both featured in the COP sequence, into regular university curricula,
> 3. credit for off-campus courses,
> 4. an on-site teaching arrangement in which university faculty and five school staff members take COP classes on alternate weeks,
> 5. student teaching credit for regular aide-level classroom work observed by university supervisors for eight weeks,
> 6. development of an ingenious field-based graduate program, generated by some of COP's first 20 graduates, in guidance and counseling administration, and

7.   institution of a graduate program in educational administration for COP graduates.

Mars Hill College of North Carolina instituted a full-year
internship in the public schools for all teacher trainees as a
result of the successful experience of the Asheville COP
participants.

Pikesville College of Kentucky, which historically trained 85
percent of the local school system's teachers, included a
greater field experience, as well as a competency-based
teacher education design, for all its students as a result of its
experience with the Pike County COP project.

Special efforts were made to include Black colleges among
the COP teacher training institutions. Particularly satisfactory collaborative relationships between white and Black
colleges were set up to serve the COP projects in Baltimore
and Nashville, among others.

As a result of the Indian Teacher Training Project (the COP
program at Humboldt State College, California), nine Native Americans had graduated by 1974 as compared with ten
Native American graduates over the past 50 years. In addition, a Native American Studies program was established
and the college hired seven Native Americans in faculty and
administrative positions, whereas in 1970, there were none.

The 36 Tempe, Arizona, COP participants who received the
baccalaureate degree in August 1974 from Arizona State
University were the largest group of Native Americans to
graduate at one time from any Arizona college or university.

A cross-cultural teacher education program was instituted at
the University of Alaska as a result of the Alaska COP-
Teacher Corps program.

Waiving of SAT cut-off scores for admissions, new courses,
credit for classroom work, reorganization of course sequences, and college faculty coming to LEA classrooms
were some of the changes in several North Carolina colleges
and universities as a result of the Winston-Salem COP
project.

As a result of their involvement with the Trenton, New Jersey, COP project, Mercer County Community College and
Trenton State College established procedures regarding

course credit transfers and sequencing of courses; new curricula were set up at MCCC; COP participants and community representatives were included in curriculum revision committees at both colleges; and a new practicum design was developed at TSC.

Inclusion of Peoria, Illinois, COP participants in classes with "regular" students at Illinois State University contributes, according to ISU faculty, to making those classes more "real" for the students.

The prestigious University of Southern California developed more flexible COP-influenced entrance requirements including:

1. Evaluation of student based on student motivation rather than grades only,
2. waiving of the Scholastic Aptitude Test,
3. allowing eight units of field work experience as a teacher aide to be included among the sixty transferable units, and
4. requirement of one semester or less of student teaching as long as the student passes the competencies required.

At the University of Arkansas, all education majors now spend a portion of their time in the Foundations course working in the public schools, following the model introduced to the University by the Fayetteville COP project.

At Oakland University, which served the Pontiac, Michigan, COP project and where half the participants made the University's Honor Roll, the School of Education, as a result of the COP experience, now requires that prior to student teaching, all students must have at least one term of internship similar to the role of the COP participant.

The EXEL (Experimental Program in Elementary Education) at Shepherd College, West Virginia, is a direct result of Shepherd's experience with the Martinsburg COP project. Indeed, the EXEL bulletin credits COP with introducing the concept of "substantial classroom experience early and continuously with methods handled in weekly seminars in lieu of the teaching block."

In Iowa, Des Moines Area Community College instituted a teacher aide program with the A.A. degree awarded after two years. The same institution now offers practicum credit to individuals in fields other than education for training achieved on the job.

Responding to the needs of the Parsons project, Kansas State College of Pittsburgh installed new courses, planned a program for training aides, and institutionalized an Administrators' Workshop on staff development.

The University of Nebraska in Lincoln saw these developments as a consequence of the local COP program:

1. public relations and communications with certain aspects of the community improved,
2. field-based courses greatly extended to meet the needs of COP participants,
3. some instructors more responsive to the needs of students—especially to those of the COP participants,
4. the faculty and staff from the University of Nebraska working with COP more aware of some of the personal problems—obstacles to learning—affecting people who have a limited income, and
5. some methods of evaluation improved as a result of the emphasis on performance and field-based experiences.

At Humboldt State University in Arcata, California, the only "recognizable" (HSU's description) Indian students on campus were the 18 in the COP Indian Teacher Education Project; long before the project concluded, there were approximately 200, and a Native American Studies Program, as well as Native American classes, had been inaugurated at HSU.

Avila College of Kansas City, Missouri, reported such changes as these:

1. block courses and short workshops offered to COP students and made available to other students and in other than the Education Department;
2. many theory courses offered after school hours at the elementary school site for COP participants and ex-

panded to on-site courses being offered at hospitals, businesses, and HEW offices by Avila College;

3. faculty for these courses, initially from Avila, now chosen from the sites themselves;

4. much more academic credit being granted for formal school and classroom experiences in all college education coursework; college working out details of a credit for Experience Program; concept already approved;

5. more independent study for responsible students;

6. for the most part, written senior year comprehensive examinations eliminated, with performance and competency-based criteria used to satisfy the graduation requirement in some cases.

Central Washington State College, the teacher training institution which served both the Tacoma and Yakima COP projects, reported these adjustments as a result of COP:

1. resident credit courses being offered locally,

2. adjusting transferable credits from other institutions,

3. registration for student teaching being held off campus,

4. post-student teaching seminar being held *prior* to student teaching,

5. COP interns making up the bulk of the student teacher load assigned to the CWSC student teacher supervisor for the Tacoma District,

6. has become more flexible in admitting candidates to teacher education from special programs, such as COP,

7. has become more flexible in endorsing students for student teaching,

8. is providing and fitting courses to the individual needs of each student, and

9. teacher education tests in math, English, reading and spelling waived for COP participants.

Whether and how many of these—and many other—solid examples of the effect of COP on colleges and universities will become permanent features at the institutions cannot yet be forecast. But substantial changes *did* take place during the life of COP, and many were clearly being introduced into the regular, post-COP behavior patterns of these institutions. For the most part, these were the colleges most in need of change. In the current jargon of accountability, the colleges provided "value added" for their COP students, and, so, too, the COP students provided "value added" to the colleges.

THE COP PARTICIPANT AS TEACHER

Evidence of the effectiveness (or, if need be, ineffectiveness) of COP-trained teachers was beginning to gather as COP concluded. Some of the accumulating data, overwhelmingly positive, is cited here.

The COP program based at the University of North Dakota, with participants from four Indian reservation communities, provided college degrees and teacher certification for 51 new teachers of American Indian origin. Virtually all returned to their communities as full-fledged teachers, thereby creating or improving those conditions:

> better relations between children and their schools,
>
> a probable slowdown in the rate of teacher turnover,
>
> teachers thoroughly attuned to and identified with the children and their problems,
>
> community pride in Indian-related attitudes, and, far from least,
>
> proof that schools with Indian children could thrive with significantly larger percentages of Indian teachers.

Of 142 degree-earning COP participants in the Chicago project, 118 became teachers in "target area" schools, that is, in schools populated by children of low-income, minority (Black and Hispanic-American) background. In Hartford, Connecticut, virtually all graduating COP aides received regular teaching posts, even in the face of a marked surplus of teachers, while 12 of the Worcester, Massachusetts project's 15 1974 graduates landed teaching positions. Of the graduates of the eight projects in Nebraska, Missouri, Iowa and Kansas, 98 percent were employed, with 44 percent of them obtaining jobs in project school districts, another nine percent in other schools, and 28 percent continuing their studies in graduate school. Typical of this region was the situation in urban Des Moines, where 28 of 39 graduates were placed as teachers in the city's schools (and two more outside the district). In Idaho, where a small but widely dispersed COP project produced 29 graduates, two-thirds became teachers in the schools the first year they were certified, and every member of the first COP graduating class in Kansas City was hired by the school system.

THE NCTL ASSESSMENTS

In July 1974, the New Careers Training Laboratory undertook an evaluation study of COP with the purpose of focusing on COP graduates serving as first-year teachers within local school districts. While each district having a COP project was responsible for an ongoing evaluation of its project, none were responsible for the evaluation of the graduate as a teacher. The resultant study, then, was the first to look at this pivotally important aspect of the Career Opportunities Program—the graduate as teacher.

Procedure

All 132 then-operating COP projects were canvassed in July 1974. Each project was requested to report the number of COP graduates, the total then employed in the district as teachers, and the school district's willingness to participate in the planned study. From the pool of 60 positive responses to an initial questionnaire and subsequent followup, 15 sites were selected to reflect the ten federal geographic regions and the diversity of COP models, and to provide some balance between urban and rural school districts.[1] The 15 sites were thus a stratified sample of the full COP universe which showed high congruence with the national COP project profile in terms of participant characteristics and project activities.

At each of the 15 sites, a sample of ten COP graduates was randomly selected from the pool of COP graduates employed there as first-year teachers. At each of the local schools where one or more of the ten COP graduates were teaching, first-year teachers who were not COP graduates were selected as a control group and matched with the COP graduates on the basis of being first-year teachers working in the same building and teaching the same grade.

Instrumentation

Data were collected along three axes: the person, the process, the product.

> *Data on the person* consisted of personal, demographic, and teacher training information, as well as those gathered by the Gordon Personal Profile and Personal Inventory and the Minnesota Teacher Attitude Inventory.
>
> *Data on the teaching process* were gathered by the use of an administrator's comparative rating scale developed by project staff, the Flanders Interaction Analysis Categories, and the Ryans Classroom Observation Record.
>
> *Data on the product*—the effect upon the student—were gathered by three instruments: the Piers-Harris Self-Concept Scale; a Parent Questionnaire designed by staff to elicit parental judgments about children's attitudes; and an individual data collection sheet which collected achievement test data on each student in the class of one of the teachers being studied, as well as information on attendance, tardiness, and disciplinary referral.

A variety of instruments along each of these axes was used to obtain a multifaceted picture of the two teacher cohorts, the COP-trained and the non-COP trained. In effect, a "Rashomon" picture was sought.

The Findings

AXIS 1 - THE PERSON.   The COP-trained teachers were older, more likely to be Black, and slightly more likely to be males as compared with the non-COP trained. (For COP and non-COP, respectively, the mean age was 35 and 26, 52% and 26% were Black, and 75% of the COP teachers were female, as were 80% of the non COP). The two groups did about as well in college, as measured by grades, although the COP-trained group expressed greater satisfaction with its college program. A higher percentage of COP-trained teachers had enrolled and planned to enroll in post-baccalaureate education.

The COP-trained teachers had more positive attitudes as expressed on all eight scales of the Gordon Personal Inventory and Personal Profile, as well as the Minnesota Teacher Attitude Inventory. The differences were significant statistically on the Gordon scales for Original Thinking, Vigor, Ascendancy, and Sociability.

AXIS 2 - THE PROCESS.   On both measures of classroom activity used in this study, the COP-trained teachers performed in a more desirable manner. In their classrooms, there was more interchange between teacher and student and the students' talk was more responsive and extended. The interaction which more frequently characterized the classrooms of the COP graduates was, according to the pertinent research, more highly correlated with positive student performance. Principals who supervised the two groups of teachers favored the COP-trained teachers in comparison with other first-year teachers they had supervised.

AXIS 3 - THE PRODUCT.   The children in the classrooms of the COP-trained teachers had a more positive self-concept, and their parents ranked their attitudes toward school more positively than did parents of children in the classrooms of the non-COP trained teachers. Although comprehensive achievement test data were not obtainable, achievement test data in which there were differences favored the children in the classrooms of the COP-trained teachers. Finally, the data regarding tardiness and disciplinary referrals were more positive for the children in the classrooms of the COP-trained teachers, while attendance data favored the non-COP trained teachers.

In sum,

> where statistically significant differences were found on each instrument as a whole, they favored the COP-trained teachers in each case;
>
> where statistically non-significant differences were found on each instrument as a whole, they favored the COP-trained teachers in each case;
>
> where statistically significant differences were found on subscales of instruments, they favored the COP-trained teachers in each case; and
>
> where statistically non-significant differences were found on subscales of instruments, they favored the COP-trained teachers in all but two cases.

The Meaning

The study found a series of consistent, although often small, more positive scores by the COP-trained teachers, as compared with the matched non-COP trained teachers in the same schools. The COP-trained teachers possessed a more favorable set of attitudes. In the classrooms, they demonstrated behaviors considered to be the more desirable ones for children's learning. Their supervisors ranked them higher. The children in their classrooms thought better of themselves and, with the exception of the score on one subscale, the children's parents believe those in the classrooms of the COP-trained teachers had better attitudes. And what slight differences there were in achievement test scores favored the COP-trained teachers' students.

It is not only this consistent set of findings but their pattern which merits attention. In comparing the classrooms of the COP-trained teachers with those of the non-COP trained, the investigators found two different teaching styles and two different student response patterns. The non-COP trained teachers engaged in more teacher-initiated interaction—lecturing and questions and short answer dialogue—while the COP-trained teachers interacted more directly with their students, elicited more and longer responses from the students, and responded more to students' comments when they arose. This more accepting and encouraging classroom behavior conduces toward more student verbal initiative, fuller responses, and more sustained interchanges. According to the pertinent research, these characteristics of classroom interaction are more desirable and correlate more highly with better student performance. The NCTL findings indicate this to be the case based on an assessment of the students' self-concept, parents' assessment of their attitudes, and their achievement.

These findings as to the success of the COP mode of teacher training were reinforced a year later. A follow-up study at the same 15 sites along Axis 1 (the person) revealed that COP-trained second year teachers were more aware than their peers of the "ethos" of the schools. Although the non-COP group was learning much about the quality and pace of school life, the COP teachers were appreciably ahead, and the gap was widening. There were also continuing pro-COP differences on pupil orientation. The COP teachers tended to be more accepting of individual differences among pupils and felt a greater sense of responsibility and accountability for the pupil's progress. The non-COP trained group tended in general to ascribe success or failure to the attitude of the pupil and failure of disciplinary action.

The follow-up assessment included two additional sites: the bilingual COP projects in Crystal City and Port Isabel, Texas. The findings in both cases paralleled those of the earlier study but with even greater differences between COP and non-COP trained teachers, notably in the areas of two-way exchanges between pupils and teachers. Even more significant were indications that, although the non-COP trained teachers at these two sites were as good as the COP trained teachers at the 15 "regular" sites, the COP ones were even better. These higher standards were attributed to the unique qualities of bilingual education.

While retaining the evaluative processes used in the first year, the second year of the NCTL examination of COP products as teachers employed a new instrument to examine a broad panorama of school/teacher/pupil data at the 17 sites. It was discovered that non-COP teachers were readier to shift schools, to another community or even state, after one year of teaching, while the COP group remained committed to their communities even though their new professional status made moving more possible than here to for. Too, the COP teachers were more inclined to (1) stay in the classroom rather than move on to allied pursuits, (2) complete a graduate degree during the next few years, and (3) retain their enthusiasm for teaching.

The second-year COP teacher, while primarily concerned with the teaching function, tended to view the school as a system and to be interested in such matters as organization, morale, teacher competence, and committee membership. By the second year, her or his non-COP peers were more concerned with such day-to-day matters as class size, modes of supervision and rules and procedures.

Subtle but important differences characterized the two groups in other areas. Both believed themselves to be competent teachers, with the non-COP teacher emphasizing an ability to sensitize pupils to be sensitive to other pupils, to show respect and to understand the home backgrounds of different types of pupils. The second-year COP graduate, on the other hand, stressed competence in obtaining the cooperation of pupils, consistency in disciplinary approaches and the capacity to interpret effectively to the pupil in a manner designed to obtain the pupil's understanding. The study further revealed that the groups simply had different attitudes toward children and their behavior. The non–COP teacher, as a rule, tended to be understanding; the COP group, on the whole, was demanding.

Finally, the COP teacher shows stronger signs of believing that, once absorbed into the local school, (s)he will be able to exert a constructive effect for needed change there. Although by no means a radical force within the school, the COP product believes that such opportunities —including those relating to work conditions, job security and collective bargaining—do exist and that they can and should be taken.

The effects of COP graduates clearly transcended even these formally assessed performances. In Ashville, North Carolina, where 24 of 27 COP "products" were employed locally as teachers, the school system anticipated less turnover on the part of Black teachers (who had traditionally sought better opportunities elsewhere) because the COP people were older and had firmer local ties. Similar beneficial by-products could be predicted, for example, in such localities as Port Isabel, Texas; Box Elder, Montana; and Tuskegee, Alabama, from all of which trained professionals in many fields historically tended to move to supposedly greener pastures.

At a different stage in the process—that of the ungraduate COP aide occupying an instructional role in the schools—there was no concerted attempt to measure effectiveness. Nor could there be. But the COP paraprofessional *was* frequently a teacher in all but name, and her (or his) effect was almost invariably positive. The line between paraprofessional and licensed teacher became blurred as familiarity stimulated respect. The result, especially in rural COP projects such as Martinsburg, West Virginia; Crystal City, Texas; Alaska; and Lewiston, Maine, among others, was that aides often took over classrooms for hours, even days and weeks, at a time. And once in the instructional seat, they brought to the children the infinite benefits of previous careers spent in non-schooling pursuits (such as fighting a war in Vietnam, as members of the New Orleans participant group had done), the sharing of experience as fellow students, and a variety of sensitivities that even the most compassionate regular teacher rarely possessed.

At the mid-way point—the third year—of its life, the Atlanta, Georgia, COP project essayed an interim judgment on how a teaching team consisting of a COP aide and "lead" teacher (plus certified reading teacher) was performing as a reading instructional group compared to a team in which the aide was not in the COP project. The average gain, unsurprisingly, was greater in every school grade from two to seven for the team with the COP participant.

Whatever the method of assessment, the form of the "cut" taken at the data, or the location of the survey, the outcome has been consistent: the COP-trained teacher is performing at least as well as, and judged by the overwhelming majority of indicators, better than her (or his) non-COP peer. This outcome is all the more remarkable when non-quantifiable social factors such as the often inadequate prior education of the COP teacher, her (or his) probably prolonged absence from formal schooling before entering (or re-entering college), and the COP participant's obligation to a full-time position while receiving academic instruction are considered.

SOME CONCLUSIONS: COP AS AN EDUCATIONAL FORCE

This report is not intended to be an assessment of the COP program (only the data on COP graduates as teachers approach definitiveness), and the conclusions cited in this section must therefore be considered as tentative and non-scientific. In reaching any conclusions, moreover, it is essential to state the initial objectives which motivate them. Five, cited often in COP literature, commend themselves as readily apparent and probably valid in the aggregate as the basic goals of the Career Opportunities Program and, therefore, as the backdrop for what follows. The five (as summarized in the excellent final report on COP of USOE Region VII) are to:

1. Attract low-income people to new careers in schools serving low-income people.
2. Find better ways of utilizing school staff through developing career lattices of positions.
3. :Encourage greater participation of parents and the community in education.
4. Find better ways of training personnel for schools through a combined classroom experience/college curriculum approach.
5. Increase cooperation between related programs and institutions.

Cutting across these lines, and generally defying rigid categorization as having been caused solely or partially by the presence of COP, are a number of tangible examples suggesting circumstances in which COP mattered. Some typical ones:

> Test data suggest that the second year of utilization of COP aides in the Little Rock, Arkansas, schools had an accelerating effect upon children's learning. The data indicate positive correlation between improved achievement and the presence of COP participants in schools. A decrease in be-

havioral problems has also been reported by teachers and principals.

Native American children in bilingual programs where COP aides were used talked more in class than a control group of Native American children not in bilingual settings. As compared with the control group, these children showed both in English and the Native language significantly less absence from school and significant increase in overall ability.

Fewer discipline problems, more individualized learning, greater opportunities for teachers to use their highest skills, and closer community involvement in the schools were reported by a principal as the effect of COP participants in the Camden, New Jersey, schools.

One hundred percent of the principals in schools where Pike County, Kentucky, COP participants worked reported that the academic performance of the children had improved as a result of COP.

There was greater achievement and improved self-image on the part of pupils in COP schools in Rochester, New York, than in comparable schools without COP participants.

Scores on the WISC were higher where COP participants were used than in comparable schools in Helena, Montana.

Comparing performance on the Metropolitan Achievement Test of similar classes of first grade children with and without COP aides in Durham, North Carolina, those with COP aides did significantly better on word knowledge, word discrimination, and reading, and slightly better in arithmetic; on all three of these subscales, those classes with COP aides scored *above* grade level, while the others scored below it. On tests for second grade children, classes with COP aides did better on four of five subscales on the MAT, while at the third grade level, classes with COP aides did better on six of eight subscales.

Principals reported improvements in discipline and learning conditions in classes where Peoria, Illinois, COP participants worked, and the parents of children in those classes reported that their children liked school more, had less difficulty, and were more eager to attend school, according to an outside evaluation.

In all grades but one, children's scores on the MAT in Atlanta, Georgia, Title I schools using COP participants were better than those Title I schools without COP participants. Only in the schools using COP participants did children progress at an annual rate of one grade per year.

In Miami, Florida, an experimental project for young children with cognitive deficits which used COP participants as the major intervention strategy in a program of sequential stimulation and development resulted in a reduction of deficits twice as great as among a control group.

That COP produced a significant number of teachers from populations heretofore little represented in the teacher force is undisputable. Their number will no doubt exceed 6,000 and their quality is likely to be at least equal to the best of the traditional new teachers. Whether they will stick to teaching, whether they will grow and become better teachers, and whether the cost was worth the product is still difficult to judge. What is clear, however, is that a federally-designed program can be mounted across the country and it can provide a means to meet an important national priority.

This goal, that of meeting a special need, was the easier of the two. More complex for assessment is the view of COP as a demonstration. Here, it may be best to look to the components of the program one-by-one and then as a whole.

Let us look, first, at the structure.

The school district as grant recipient. There is no doubt that the scheme of funding the local school district and having it subcontract for services with the colleges and universities was successful. While it may have been possible to achieve the desired relationships between practitioner preparer and practitioner employer in some other way, the scheme adopted achieved the desired goal with few, if any, negative consequences.

The teacher training institution as partner in the in-service development of the school's staff. While the colleges and universities were able to adapt to meet COP's needs, there continue to be limits as to their ability to be full participants in this process. Perhaps it is inappropriate to see them in such a role; rather, it may be that there will always need to be a mediating force, such as a COP project between the school district and the university.

The triad of school-college-community in a parity relationship. Clearly, all played a part at various levels of COP. What is made clear by the COP experience in this regard is that the roles of the three are not the same; that they vary by function and over time; that in contrast to the other two, the community both is more amorphous and lacking in an ongoing discrete set of functions and thus there is a tendency for it to be left by the wayside or to be involved only episodically; and that the continuing effective involvement of all three requires effort and expense.

The role of the state coordinator. The experience here is so divergent as to preclude any overall conclusions. Where done well, the state coordinator functions served significantly to abet program success. On the other hand, in some states, programs achieved high levels of success with little, if any, state involvement. Whether greater involvement would have led to higher degrees of success (or permanence) is not clear.

The role of the federal government. Having been the handiwork of powerful USOE leadership, COP soon was largely left to fend for itself. To a limited extent, it did this successfully. It was served well, by and large, by the middle-echelon officials who were responsible for it following its launching. The dispersal of federal project offices to the regions was a positive step, especially in the light of the frequent inability of Washington-based staff to travel and the penchant for staff reorganizations from which the staff in the regions were largely immune (or, at least, less effected).

Turning from structure to substance, we can focus on the COP participant, as worker and as student, and the interaction between the two roles. As a worker, the arrangement of having salaries paid from a program source did little to hamper the COP program and, of course, stretched its dollars. As workers, COP participants provided yet additional evidence as to the usefulness and effectiveness of paraprofessionals. As students, they enjoyed a high level of success.

It is at the point of overlap between these roles that tensions arise. That which is most appropriate for a worker to be doing on the job is not necessarily the most instructive for the person who views the job as an experiential part of their professional preparation. Similarly, that which is most valuable in a course for a student or a practitioner-to-be is not necessarily the most useful at the moment for someone who is seeking help in meeting job requirements. All this is to say that the problems inherent in seeking to combine work and study, to integrate theory and practice, have not been solved in COP. In an ideal situation, there is need for many "mores"—more preparation of the teacher with whom the participant works; more opportunities for school people to have a chance to reflect and think; more chances for participants to enjoy experiences beyond their job—to work in or, at least, visit schools other than their own, to try things out without the pressures of the classroom, to spend time in college courses irrelevant to their work. In addition, more attention was needed to the personal burdens of participants and their families. Little thought was given, for example, to the tensions produced in a middle-aged, working class family when the wife gains an education, college degree and higher status job, to say nothing of an avalanche of attention and praise for her achievement.

What will remain? Of course, there will be the thousands of COP participants whose lives have been changed forever, both individually and as teachers. And, as a result, there will be the tens of thousands of children, both the natural ones of these participants and the pupils whom they will affect over their years as teachers, who will be changed.

There is the experience of a program which recognized the capability people had if only they were given the opportunity to develop and display it. This offers lessons

for the establishment of public service employment programs; for the setting of job qualifications based upon what
a person can do; for the establishing of personnel procedures which emphasize "selecting in" and then training,
rather than "screening out"; for the rejection of the myth
that all is set in a person's life at a very young age; for the
establishment of new criteria of "college material"; for new
indices of performance.

Institutionally, there are the particular changes in individual school systems and colleges, as well as the broader
effect on statewide programs (Ohio, West Virginia, and
Florida, among others), and on the general world of higher
education for those other-than-the-middle-class white
youth in residential programs. So, too, there is the change
in the mode of the preparation of teachers—changes which
emphasize ongoing exposure to practice, simultaneous integration of work and study, the use of teams in instruction
and learning, and the development of curricula suitable for
a multicultural world.

The hard data that *are* available, mostly the information developed from such sources as the study of COP
graduates as teachers, lead to different kinds of examples
and conclusions.

First, and overall, it is evident that low-income adults,
long away from formal education, can be recruited successfully to work in the schools, can do that work with benefit
to children, can combine that work with successful performance as college students, and, as a result, can become
effective teachers of low-income children. In sum, the concept of the Career Opportunities program is one which can
be and, in this instance, has been successful.

In an assessment of COP midway in its course, Dr.
William Smith, successor to Dr. Don Davies as Associate
Commissioner of USOE's Bureau of Educational Personnel Development, labeled COP a "mid-range demonstration," an effort which brought together a series of program

ideas found successful in earlier more limited efforts, which sought to demonstrate the potential in their combination and expansion. Among earlier ideas brought together in COP was the broad "new careers" concept which asserted that persons recruited from among the poor, when simultaneously provided jobs, training, and education, could become a new kind of professional. In a sense, COP is an expression of that concept.

More specifically, COP took up ideas such as: the potential of paraprofessionals to make a direct contribution to the delivery of human services, in this instance to the learning of low-income children; the usefulness of staff differentiation designs, particularly when combined with career advancement; the value of combining both work and study; the field-based focus of teacher education; and the involvement in relationships built upon parity of all the central parties (viz. school, university, and community people) to the professional preparation enterprise. While it is premature to make judgments as to the relative efficacy of particular parts of the COP design, the overall findings do indicate that the COP principles have worked. That is, it has recruited, selected, trained, and graduated low-income adults who have, probably far more often than not, become successful teachers of low-income children.

At a time when teacher vacancies are fewer, it becomes all the more crucial that the persons employed as teachers perform well. In addition, given the public investment in teacher education, it is important that the persons so trained do become and remain teachers. Already with roots in their community, COP-trained teachers are more likely to remain there and to remain in teaching.

What is most essential is the recognition that among the vast pool of low-income adults are many persons, who, given realistic opportunities in a carefully designed program, can make powerful social contributions, in this instance, as teachers. As programs to staff the schools are developed, as plans to train persons to become teachers materialize, indeed, as persons are recruited to higher education at large, the potential of low-income, frequently minority adults, long absent from formal school but powered by their own motivation in the context of realistic opportunity, should not be ignored. The issue is not whether the Career Opportunities Program, as such, should be done again—although few such efforts have been as successful. It is the program intent, the program design, and the program ethos which warrant extension and development.

For a program never mentioned in the legislation which made it possible, early left to fend for itself in a political climate not at all sympathetic to its ethos and efforts, and complicated to run at the local level, COP seems to have done well; most of all because of the power of the people whose ambition and energy it was able to tap, but, also, because of the effective administration at the operational level and the intrinsic power of its design.

NOTES

1. Miami, Florida;
   Richmond, Virginia;
   Gary, Indiana;
   Grand Rapids, Michigan;
   Kansas City, Missouri;
   Tempe, Arizona;
   Helena, Montana;
   Tacoma, Washington;
   San Antonio, Texas;
   Los Angeles, California;
   Chipley, Florida;
   Lewiston, Maine;
   Newark, New Jersey;
   Seattle, Washington;
   New Orleans, Louisiana.

Chapter 10

AN ANALYSIS AND PERSPECTIVE

Arthur Pearl

It is difficult to evaluate the impact that paraprofessionals have had on education over the past decade because the field has gone through so many cataclysmic shocks. However, where serious school reform is undertaken paraprofessionals will play a vital role in (1) reestablishing the credibility of the public school, (2) reestablishing the credibility of the school of education, (3) developing the power of the consumer in education, and (4) establishing fiscal priorities and adequate funding for current as well as future education programs. To make this case, however, it is first necessary to review the current situation.

RISE OF THE PARAPROFESSIONAL

The paraprofessional has been a factor in education since the institutionalization of the schooling process. Only recently has teaching transcended a paraprofessional status. In recent decades, however, a new category of teacher has been established to fill the vacuum between the ordained professional and the teacher that historically was held in such low regard. This newly created paraprofessional has characteristics that distinguish her from the professional (s)he is designed to assist. Unlike the professional, (s)he tends to be poor, nonwhite, and often non-English speaking. (S)he is hired to provide resources and understanding that the professional does not have, and (s)he brings to the school a relationship with the community that the commuting teacher lacks the time, sponsorship, and predilection to establish. The paraprofessional is a mechanism to fulfill affirmative action, bilingual, and community action responsibilities. (S)he is simultaneously many things and nothing. To attain this lofty (or lowly) station, the paraprofessional has undergone many changes and has been employed with many different understandings.

In Bay City, Michigan, an experiment begun in 1953 with funds from the Ford Foundation is a landmark in the use of less than professionally credentialed teachers. In this experiment teachers were paired with aides who were hired to relieve them of menial or clerical duties. These aides were high school graduates and conformed in style and deportment to community standards. In other words, they were similar to the teachers they were hired to assist. In two years of experimentation, the aides were unable to produce more scholastic achievement, as measured by standardized tests, but parents and students judged them to be useful. The Bay City experiment was not universally applauded; some parents believed that the use of paraprofessionals in the schooling process undermined educational standards, and some teachers believed that the use of paraprofessionals threatened their hard-won salaries. The Bay City experiment had a minimal effect on school staffing patterns, and the paraprofessional did not achieve real prominence until the mid-1960s, with the emergence of the antipoverty and civil rights programs.

Two features of the antipoverty program gave impetus to the hiring of paraprofessionals. The most important feature was the notion that the poor were poor because they lacked desperately needed services and that once they were able to compete on an equal footing with the affluent, poverty would end. Supplying these services required staff that would exhaust the short supply of professionally trained practitioners. The rationale of all this was that a rapidly expanding economy would create ever expanding opportunities and allow anyone who was adequately trained to enter the growing ranks of teachers, physicians, engineers, social workers, scientists, and so on.[1] Through a variety of legislative actions such as the Economic Opportunity Act, the Elementary and Secondary School Act, and the Vocational Educational Act of 1963, a boom occurred in the paraprofessional field, and hundreds of thousands of persons—mostly low-income, nonwhite, and female—were employed in the field of education.

In addition to the notion of creating employment for the poor, the early War on Poverty was characterized by the related idea of maximum feasible participation. This philosophy had two logical outlets: community residents should be represented on policy-making boards and should be employed in community service. These outlets were compatible, and the existence of school boards dominated by low-income persons facilitated the employment of those who lacked training or experience as teacher aides and the like.

The paraprofessional boom did not last long, however. By the end of the sixties, the flush optimism had given way to resignation. Community boards had confronted established political systems and had been routed. Programs stagnated because funds were siphoned from the War on

Poverty to the war in Vietnam. A new administration not only catered to but manufactured hostility among Middle Americans toward the undeserving poor, which led to a congressional reluctance to appropriate new funds and allowed the president to impound most of the funds that had been appropriated on the grounds that the programs were inefficient or unproductive. The surge in the need for professionals was not forthcoming, and the supply of certified teachers exceeded the number of available openings. Teachers effectively improved their bargaining status and obtained salary increases and other benefits that ate into diminishing reserves, thus eroding the financial base for hiring paraprofessionals.

The decline of the paraprofessional movement was reflected not only in unemployment but in the sacrifice of the early appeal and plan for career advancement. Programs to assist paraprofessionals in obtaining credentials (e.g., the Scheuer Amendment to the Economic Opportunity Act, the Career Opportunities Program in the Educational Professions Development Act, and Supplementary Training in Head Start) were reduced in scale and aspiration, enthusiasm within school systems waned, and a sizable constituency in professional associations was replaced by ever more recalcitrant opposition.

Paraprofessionals continue to exist in education. Although some programs have been reduced, other modest developments have taken their place. For example, the current emphasis on bilingual education has stimulated employment, among Spanish- and Chinese-speaking paraprofessionals especially, and the demands of affirmative action have also kept the need for teacher aides and other assistants alive, albeit tenuously. Rarely do these individuals have the security of tenure, their salaries almost always come from funds that can dry up at a moment's notice, and they have no clear prospects for the future.

DECLINE OF EDUCATION

Not so long ago, there was one clear way to distinguish a conservative from a progressive (liberal, even radical): his stance toward education. The conservative took a dim view of education while the progressives enthusiastically supported it. The conservatives characteristically complained that education cost too much. He was especially antagonistic toward spending money on anything but the basics and viewed everything else as frills. He was especially suspicious of any aspect of education that might instill subversive notions about God and country.

On the other hand, the expansion of education was central to almost all leftist thinking. One of the ten measures that Karl Marx advocated for advancing the revolutionary potential of the proletariat was free education for all children in public schools, which of course was related to the exploitative practice of using child labor. Although conservatives maintained their attack on education, they now find curious allies in self-proclaimed radicals. A series of devastating "cheap shots" wracked education as group after group came forth with calls to free children from imprisonment of schooling.[2] In a belated response to the absurd claim that education could, by remediating all deficits, be the mediating force to eliminate inequity in the United States, the "antischoolers" took an equally absurd tack: that the schools were corrupt beyond reform; they perpetuated racial, class, and sexual biases; they were impersonal institutions that herded children like animals; they blocked creativity, personal liberty, and psychological liberation; and they reflected all the sordidness and oppressiveness of the greater society. Therefore, only by putting an end to schooling could freedom be achieved.

Thus the 1960s saw the emergence of a clique—composed of John Holt, Jonathan Kozal, Peter Maris, and Ivan Illich, who were allied at times with Christopher Jencks,

Charles Reich, and Theodore Roszak—calling for an end to schooling. And even when it was pointed out to them that the schools were actually weak and relatively unimportant institutions, the antischoolers argued that liberating children from schools was the first step toward total deinstitutionalization. They presented their argument without data or sequential logic and expected it to stand on its own merits—as unquestionable as the assertion that a hair cut would lead inexorably to decapitation.

This article is not devoted to the shabby scholarship and irresponsibility of the antischoolers; it deals with the undeniable fact that the combined assault of old conservatives and new radicals; the undeniable failure of schools to deal effectively with racial and sex biases (few nonwhites joined the antischool clamor); the undeniable inability of schools to enlist the loyalty of students, parents, and other new constituencies; and the decline in the number of school-aged children meant that the paraprofessional movement achieved prominence at a time when the credibility of schooling had plummeted to its nadir.

THE PARAPROFESSIONAL'S PLACE IN THE FUTURE OF EDUCATION

Credibility of the Public School

No serious discussion about the future of paraprofessionals in education can take place unless it includes proposals for reestablishing the credibility of public education. Now that the romantic cloud created by both the pro- and antischoolers is lifting, we find ourselves immersed in enormously complex problems, which cannot be solved by any privileged elite. Solutions will require the active support of an enlightened electorate. It should be obvious that calls for total allegiance to experts lack force and that unless citizens have a general understanding of the goals of economic, environmental, and other programs, these programs will be sabotaged. In fact, if the last 30 years have taught us anything, it is that there is enormous political success in attacking the college-trained expert. Joe McCarthy gained a measure of prominence during the late 1940s and early 1950s by attacking the "eggheads." During the 1960s and 1970s Ronald Reagan and Richard Nixon carried on this traditional attack on intellectuality that has served others so well. This is especially true today because any proposed solution that promises to solve international conflict, ecological imbalance, poverty, and sexual and racial inequality simultaneously will require considerable changes in the life-style, values, priorities, diet, and aspirations of almost everyone, and the average American is not about to give up everything (s)he has worked so hard for unless convinced that the sacrifice is necessary and that (s)he can obtain gratification in other ways. This cannot be done without education, and education cannot be obtained unless paraprofessionals are in leadership roles.

Why is the revitalization of education—or schooling—necessary? And why are paraprofessionals vital to this restoration? Critics of the left and right were only partially responsible for undermining confidence in public education. Teachers and administrators completed the job. Again, the left and right were conspirators. The right insulted students' intelligence by striving for no more than basic literacy, while the left insulted their intelligence by urging them to do their own thing. The net result was a population that was incapable of dealing conceptually with any problem. The only type of education that is defensible is one that treats significant problems significantly. To treat a problem significantly, students must be able to (1) describe phenomena adequately and debate the validity of different descriptions, (2) analyze the reasons for the phenomena, and (3) most important, propose feasible solutions to problems.

To tackle the problem of racism, for example, students must be able to debate descriptions of racism that range from systems that discriminate against nonwhites to those that posit the problem in terms of genetic or other deficiencies that nonwhites bring to the system. Because different descriptions lead to distinctively different analyses, those who believe that racism is related to institutional problems will identify institutional factors that produce inequality. Those who believe that racism is related to genetic deficiencies will present data that demonstrate the intellectual inferiority, social instability, and lack of stimulation of nonwhites. These different analyses will lead to fundamentally different solutions. Those who are system oriented will advocate changes in the educational system (e.g., heterogeneous groups, affirmative action, new curricula) and changes outside the schools (e.g., increased employment opportunities, and the like). Those who are deficit-oriented will offer proposals for remedial education, head starts in schools, and the like. These two systems of thought must be debated throughout the schooling process. Young children should learn about the different theses by listening to teachers debate and question both viewpoints. Older children should actively engage in the debates and formulate and test theses both in school and nonschool settings. Older students must defend any proposal in the context of other constraints on social planning: e.g., finite energy resources, economic considerations, knowledge of human potential, and political strategies that are needed to make a proposal a reality. Those who argue that the existing system requires racism must devise a system that does not require it; they must design wage policies and methods of distributing wealth that do not make inequality an integral part of the economic structure. As students become more sophisticated, they must be prepared to discuss Phillip's thesis that true full employment leads to a breakdown in the stability of money, the growth thesis that progress requires more and more technical development, the pros and cons of "meritocracies," and so forth and indicate how all these factors influence relationships between races, socio-economic classes, and sexes in the United States and the world.

No student should be given a college degree unless (s)he can propose and defend as feasible a solution to war, environmental destruction, poverty, racism, and dehumanizing social organizations. This type of education is a far cry from the trivia and passivity imposed on students by current schooling and from the irrelevance of no schooling at all. But no other kind of schooling is defensible! The establishment of a vibrant educational system will demand educational leadership beyond anything asked for in the past. And it is here that the topic of the paraprofessional's significance in education becomes relevant. The paraprofessional must take on this new role simply because the professional teacher cannot do so. Teachers as a group are not in a position to exercise true educational leadership for many reasons. The most important one is that their background and experience are restricted and they have characteristically been concerned with elevation of self. Rarely have they participated in important struggles against war or social injustice. Their organizations reflect protectionism without ideological coherence. Thus teachers' organizations stress all the selfishness of professionalism and corrupted trade unionism without balancing concerns for improvement of the educational process.

Therefore, their pious pronouncements about commitment to students too often merely mask a call for higher wages and better working conditions.

Another reason why established teachers are unable to lead educational reform is that logistically they are located outside the constituency they must lead. Teachers are not members of the communities that are demanding educational change. The fact that teachers commuted to and from the Oceanhill-Brownsville section of Brooklyn, New

York, led directly to the teacher-community conflict there, which even today smolders and impedes the formation of coalitions that are necessary for true change.

This does not mean that paraprofessionals are mobilized for educational change. Unfortunately, they are politically weak and conceptually disorganized. But they have the *potential* to exercise leadership because they cannot step outside of ongoing conflict and because they are members of the community. Anyone who has worked in the New Careers programs has been impressed by the energy of the New Careerists as well as overwhelmed by the challenge of focusing that energy. The paraprofessional, far more than the professional, is incensed by institutional inequities, is allied with students and parents, and is a part of grass-roots political movement. These factors make her a key to educational reform.

The teacher cannot be ignored in educational change. A substantial percentage (albeit a minority) of teachers are dedicated, heroically and totally, to educational change, but they will be successful only if they are allied with paraprofessionals and consumers of education. Again, paraprofessionals are crucial because they provide both physical support to forward-looking teacher leadership and links to vitally necessary political support. In other words, educational change will require new alliances. These alliances will be formed among a fraction of teachers, paraprofessionals, and others. A movement that is dominated by paraprofessionals is doomed to fail because it is romantically antiintellectual. A movement that is dominated by teachers is doomed to fail because of its elitism. A movement that is dominated by consumers of education is the most unreal romantic notion of all because it reduces the workers in the system to menial functionaries who must attempt to implement policies that are conceived by persons who do not even have the responsibility to ascertain whether their policies are desirable or feasible.

The paraprofessional needed for educational renewal is a far different person doing far different things than historically has been the case. The paraprofessional we have known has been assigned to mentally stultifying tasks, manipulated and used to pacify or control dissident students, and asked to function as an undercover agent for an oppressive administration. The established authorities who formulate these roles are not consciously malicious. They simply view the roles as a means of maintaining equilibrium in a system that has the allegiance and support of its professionals and other staff. In other words, they are as dedicated to the idea that the existing educational system is healthy for children as were those well-meaning people who not so long ago recommended heroin as a nonaddictive cure for morphine addiction.

The new paraprofessional must provide an intellectual presence—assisting in the development of an ever evolving consciousness by (1) presenting herself as a model of a coherent, thinking person, (2) structuring major abstract problems into concrete projects of increasing complexity so that students will not be overwhelmed by the enormity of current crises, and (3) facilitating discussion and analysis of students' experiences. The new paraprofessional not only has a different job to do, (s)he must work with persons of varying ages. Currently, paraprofessionals usually work with young children because older students require more than the primitively educated paraprofessional is prepared to give. In the future the paraprofessional will work with all age groups; the greatest number will work with adults, and adult education will become the largest and most important segment of educational activity.

The new paraprofessional cannot assume a vital role in a new educational system unless (s)he is properly educated and trained. This fact presents yet another challenge to education—a challenge to the school of education.

Reestablishing the Credibility of the School of Education

The most bankrupt element of our educational system is the school of education. Even in the heyday of schooling, the education that teachers obtained was not impressive. Prospective teachers were subjected to philosophical-sounding gibberish that was not designed to be implemented and some training in low-level skills. In essence, they learned a little vocabulary, some orientation toward school manners and customs, and illusory feelings of competence. Classes in the school of education were so dull and unchallenging that they succeeded in discouraging intellectually active people from striving for credentials and thereby tended to limit the number of dangerous, subversive types in teaching.

Schools of education have contributed significantly to the decline of the importance of schooling because of their almost total lack of intellectuality. As the crisis of the public schools has deepened, schools of education have retreated into even more indefensible positions and activities. Although the two paths this retreat has taken appear at first glance to be different, their consequences have been identical. One path that schools of education have taken is to train teachers to teach specific skills—i.e., they have reduced teaching to a set of prescribed behaviors and reduced learning to a set of prescribed performances. As an unthinking technician, the teacher is relieved of responsibility for creating true understanding of and formulating solutions to major problems. His theoretical guide consists of a simplistic and mechanistic behaviorism which he is asked to accept as dogma. The retreat to mindless technology characterizes most of current teacher training.

The second, seemingly opposite path is the infatuation with open classrooms, which are designed to liberate the children by encouraging their natural curiosity. The result has been rhetorical nonsense that oversimplifies all problems, demeans intellectual discipline, and is guided by a simplistic humanistic psychology that the teacher is asked to accept as dogma.

The nostalgic retreat to rousseauism relieves the teacher of any responsibility for formulating feasible solutions to major social problems. The retreat to sanctuaries for children characterizes almost everything that is not highly technical. Because the ideas of both camps are so unreal, because the school of education is so remote from actual teaching problems, and because the students have had so few outside experiences, it is possible for persons to embrace *both* seemingly contradictory irrelevancies.

There is no way out for schools of education except to bring them into the actual schooling process. In the old days, this was done in experimental schools, which rightfully ran their course. Perhaps experimental schools should be reinstituted on a limited basis. But the true revitalization of teacher education must come with the paraprofessional.

The notion that education and experience should be coordinated was enunciated by Pearl and Riessman in *New Careers for the Poor* (1964), which offered the following alternative to the notion that the poor had to be served. Poverty would be overcome only if the poor had the opportunity to serve: i.e., persons with limited skills, training, and experience could be put to work first, and through a combination of the best of formal education and the best of apprenticeship learning, they could learn to take greater responsibilities. History has proved that our assumptions about the existence of talent among the poor were sound and that persons who had been relegated to enforced uselessness, denigrated as lazy, stupid, and without social worth had proved themselves capable. But the vision of new careers for the poor never became a reality, partially because agencies were unable or unwilling to develop new career ladders, but, most important, because universities and colleges would not make the necessary changes. Rather than incorporate the best features of education and apprenticeship, most New Careers programs adopted the worst features of the two approaches to professional development. On the job, the New Careerists learned to be like the irrelevant practitioner; in college they were subjected to homilies and useless metaphors that were advertised as theory. In retrospect, New Careers should have focused more on university reform. Without such reforms it is doubtful that we can survive current and future shocks.

Colleges and universities are handicapped by their admission policies. Not only is the college student drawn disproportionately from a narrow spectrum of the population (e.g., middle-income, white, male), he is drawn from a narrow age group (18 to 25) with extremely limited experience. He is then secluded in the university—and let out occasionally to visit family and friends and to have some field experiences in much the same way a prisoner is furloughed. And, upon graduation, he is asked to serve populations he does not know—and fears because they look and act different—and to exercise leadership in situations such as violent confrontation, extortion, drug traffic, prostitution, and the like that were never even contemplated in the school of education in which he had matriculated.

Paraprofessionals can force variety on schools of education. Paraprofessionals do not become teachers by going to college; they become teachers by having college come to them. The paraprofessional does not need to be told what the problems are, she is already immersed in them. This does not mean that she is loath to buy cheap solutions or solutions that maintain inequality; she simply knows there is a problem.

Paraprofessionals give to schools of education a needed vitality through their range of experiences, class backgrounds, and ages. Furthermore, they cannot, for a variety of reasons, take on the arrogance of the typical college student, who "knows" that he will succeed because he is sensitive, loving, and free and that those who are currently teaching fail because they are none of those things.

The paraprofessional needs an intellectually alive school of education if (s)he is to continue to grow in consciousness and responsibility. The school of education needs the kind of maturity and experience that the paraprofessional has to offer if educational training is to become relevant. Therefore, we must mandate that at least 50 per cent of all students in schools of education must be paraprofessionals. We must revise our system of credentials so that it provides a legally established, logical sequence of licenses ranging from teacher aide to intermediate professional to master teacher.

Any call for increased employment in public service must have attached to it funds that will not only enable the paraprofessional to continue up the career ladder but enable the school of education to institute necessary, fundamental changes. The hoaxes of behaviorism and the open classroom must be replaced by the kind of true intellectual presence demanded by today's complexities. The paraprofessional, forced to be a flunky in the past, will become a key factor in education, and the ability of faculty in schools of education to reach out to and form a partnership with him or her is likely to determine the viability of our future.

Developing the Power of Consumers of Education

As education fails in general, specific groups emerge with narrow concerns to meet special exigencies. Thus some white parents have tried to create schools which continue to teach children that God made whites superior, while other white parents created alternatives that catered to the natural curiosity of their creative children. Some black parents called for schools that dealt more specifically, and certainly more favorably with the black experience. Some view these alternatives as important, progressive movements, which came into being as a consequence of the personal liberation movements of the 1960s and therefore are harbingers of more important developments yet to come.

These developments are not positive. On the contrary, they represent a serious retreat and are basically reactionary. The personal liberation movements were not true underclass movements: many of the issues involved in the civil rights, minority, and women's liberation movements were middle-class oriented. These movements did not formulate visions of social reorganization that would eliminate inequality or oppression. At best they sought to rearrange poverty and inequality; at worst they chose to ignore social problems. Because of their class basis and isolated emphases and their concerns with small communes, small group encounters, and *local* control over institutions, these movements became obsessed with the symptoms of a sick society. They never addressed root causes. For example, advocates of the movement for local control can be compared to a group of cells that demands local control over the horse's tail without regard for the horse. Therefore, these movements were precisely the same as the petty bourgeoisie efforts to sustain self that Karl Marx, in his manifesto described as reactionary, not revolutionary, because "they try to roll back the wheel of history." Clearly, the dominant theme of the 1960s was a return to a more simplistic way of social and personal life. These movements were unpolitical at a time when all change had to be political. They were metaphysical at a time when all calculations had to be within the limitations of finite earth. They were separatist and fragmented at a time when all solutions had to be integrated and coherent. They were nonideological at a time when we needed new coordination of thought processes. They were clearly reactionary in the sense that the beneficiaries were indisputably the most retrogressive of our political elements—it was a period when Richard Nixon, Ronald Reagan, and George Wallace could rise to prominence while the Joe Clarks, Ernest Gruenings, and Wayne Morses were retired from political life.

No politics is not new politics, and playing with words will not make it otherwise. The 1960s brought about an even further decline of organized labor and pitted natural allies against each other; the progressive nature of the third estate—the cities—was neutralized by fiscal crises that left the cities at the mercy of federal funding. And even worse, the decline of political instruction meant the decline of political consciousness. It was a period of instant movements, TV-created folk heros, and government-created revolutionaries. Those who insist that the 1960s brought personal if not political liberation cite the opening up to public debate of intimate, private feelings in staged encounters and the opening up to public exhibition of the naked human body, sex in various combinations and positions, and other subjects that were previously taboo. Neither their evidence nor their logic is convincing. In the author's opinion, people were less liberated at the end of the sixties than they were at the beginning. The breakdown of social taboos is not evidence of freedom, it is evidence of the spiritual and personal decline that Durkheim defined as anomie. The infatuation with nakedness and open sex was a frank admission by our newly liberated population that they were incapable of contemplating anything more intellectually challenging. The new liberated student regressed to infancy; like many infants, he believed that by stamping his foot, he could command adult status. Greater dependency, rather than greater freedom, is reflected in the ever increasing use of drugs and the greater likelihood of being the victim of violence, becoming a convert to any of the hundreds of new "religions," and being narcotized by the mass media (television has become the opiate of the people), as evidenced by fads in clothing, hair styles, preferences in music—all of which were fleeting. Even in the area of personal relations, claims of liberation were grossly exaggerated. Because thought and theory had been rejected, individuals confused license with freedom, insensitivity and bad manners with liberation, irresponsibility with courage, and self-indulgence with social concern. They were infatuated with violence that militated against any true personal liberation; everything about the decade was violent but especially its metaphor. It was the decade of the bully and romanticized sloth and sloppiness. The children of the rich enjoyed making their parents miserable. Middle-class youth were liberated from work by illegitimately opting for welfare, and they did so without recognizing the dependency implicit in that action. The so-called ecology movement was a complete sham; it was simply another opportunity for the well entrenched to sneer at working men and women, just as the women's movement was an indirect slap at working and nonwhite women. The prison reform movement made heros out of rapists and murderers; the fact that many prisoners are the unfortunate victims of racial and class injustice and other oppressive conditions does not make them heros or likely leaders of reform or revolutionary movements.

The so-called movements of the 1960s sapped a society of its energy and humor and splintered potential coalitions. Coalition became a dirty word in the sixties. Every form of irresponsibility was fostered, and the evidence for this contention is overwhelming—crimes against people and property, venereal disease, and environmental destruction increased; the cities deteriorated; wealth and power were concentrated in fewer hands; and there was no sustained antithetical organization. The only evidence for liberation was personal testimony, which was similar to the testimony that Billy Graham or a seller of quack cancer cures is able to solicit. And Billy Graham and cancer quacks outperformed the new liberators in gaining converts.

The fact that the sixties represented a dismal regression in the struggle for liberation was a direct result of the failure of education.[3] Students regressed to infantile negativism because their teachers defaulted on their responsibility. The schools responded to student revolt by becoming even more irresponsible. Control was the key issue in all school activities, which is additional evidence of denial of liberation.

In this deteriorating situation, people clutched one straw after another. Many clutched the straw of consumerism. Consumerism fits nicely into the illusion of personal liberation. The consumer does not need to be involved in the difficult problem of planning, governance, or policymaking. He does not have to work through all the complexities of production. All he needs to do is withhold purchase and by doing so influence production. The innocence of this position is exceeded only by its arrogance. In education the consumer movement gained prominence in a variety of forms. Community control of schools was one mechanism to give the consumer more power; alternative and free schools also were predicated on consumer power. Books were published that told parents and students how to grab power in existing institutions. During the 1960s many educational enterprises were established with the consumer in control. But there is no evidence that the schooling under these auspices produced students who were better able to deal with social problems than did the oppressive schools that they replaced. In fact, schools never believed that this was their responsibility.

The consumer movement gained as the producer (labor) movement waned. When traditional movements lose their dynamism, people naturally look elsewhere for leadership. The consumer movement was viewed as a resource for political revival. Conservatives such as Ralph Nader were proclaimed as leaders of the future because they exposed the perfidy of auto and drug manufacturers, but they have never come forth with a plan for a new society that does not require built-in obsolescence. But more important, Nader and other consumer advocates refuse to recognize the limitations of consumer power.[4]

In a good society, consumer power is essential. Consumers should exercise influence over human services particularly through a variety of political activities such as membership on policy-making boards and the like. Organized consumers have an extremely important role to play in determining whether the society is providing a good life for all its citizens. But the key to a good society is not the consumer but the *producer*. The consumer can be a constructive critic and ally, but he cannot be allowed to tyrannize the work force.

The consumer movement was the direct result of the corruption of the producer (organized labor) by its consumerism and the corruption of the human service worker by its professionalism. It was logical to look to the consumer when old heros failed, but what is logical is not necessarily possible or desirable. The consumer can be a power in education, but only if the paraprofessional attains responsibility in education. The paraprofessional in education, because (s)he is a consumer, is more likely than is the professional to be for the consumer and more likely to be an ally in political activity with the consumer. Therefore, (s)he can facilitate the development of real power for the consumer. For the term consumer power to rise above empty slogan, the consumer must (1) be involved in educational services, (2) be able to remove the mystery from educational programs and practices, (3) participate in planning activities, and (4) be able to articulate a cogent and coherent philosophy. The paraprofessional (or new professional) is the essential ingredient in this formula.

1.   *The role of the consumer and the paraprofessional in educational services.* In education as in all human service, the

consumer—the student—participates significantly in the service. But the extent of participation is severely limited. A self-educated person is perhaps slightly better off than a person who is not educated at all. The exaggerated importance of the consumer is yet another form of the virulent anti-intellectualism championed by Robert Theobold, who in his proposal for a guaranteed annual income argued that human service can be handled through voluntary arrangements. Although some aspects of education can be negotiated by loose relationships such as these, if that is the ultimate, then education will continue to wallow in trivial, extraneous matters. A genuine education requires far more challenging and significant learning than is attempted in self-help and voluntary systems. The meaningful involvement of the consumer requires leadership, and that leadership must be provided on an ongoing, consistent, central, *and paid* basis. Only persons who work as teachers can provide that leadership. Only paraprofessionals are prepared to move into that responsibility, for all the reasons that already have been advanced. A relevant education requires a tight and focused organization. The consumer cannot monopolize that organization because (s)he is only transiently connected with it. Therefore, unless the energy of teachers is used to build this organization, consumer input will be hollow and illusory. The consumer becomes a power in education only when the teachers, the organization, and consumers work as a genuine partnership.

2.   *The role of the consumer and the paraprofessional in removing the mystery from schooling.* The consumer's powerlessness in education is maintained to a large extent by the secret codes and other indecipherable actions of professionals. Relatively simple activities, such as the teaching of reading, are confounded and obscured by contrived language and complicated paraphernalia. The consumer is overwhelmed by this and must retreat. They gain power, however, as the mystery is taken out of these procedures. And here again, the paraprofessional is the key.

3.   *The role of the consumer and the paraprofessional in the planning process.* Because education is not a simple process, it can never gain credibility through inertia or retreat. A new kind of education must be planned. Education planned by teachers alone is likely to continue along the path to oblivion. Education planned by consumers alone is likely to be a fairy tale. Primary planning must come from knowledgeable producers. Consumer power in this instance is maintained through continued negotiation, which survives the oblivion of both elitism and romanticism through the development of a consumer-oriented paraprofessional.

4.   *The role of the consumer and the paraprofessional in developing an adequate educational philosophy.* Consumer power is a function of consumer consciousness. Knowing what is wrong is not synonymous with true praxis. Only when the consumer can propose sound programs can there be true consumer power, and that can only happen in conjunction with teachers who are in the vanguard.

Establishing Fiscal Priorities and Adequate Funding for Current and Future Programs

Paraprofessionals gained importance in education as new funds were made available to education, and they lost importance as funds were drained away. An increased investment in education is critical to the society's survival. Unless there are alternative places to put money, it is impossible to withdraw support from indefensible and destructive investments such as military hardware, highway construction, and subsidy of a variety of goods producing industry. Increased funds are necessary in education because without these funds the development of new approaches to education, especially adult education, will be impossible. Here, of course, lies the Catch 22 of education. Without new funds, education cannot be credible, and unless it is credible, education cannot obtain new funds. Professional teachers could gain some funds with slightly more accountability, but certainly not the amounts that are needed. Education must, in the near future, represent at least 10 per cent of the economic activity in the United States. This means that at least eight million people should be paid to teach full-time in place of the four million or so who are now paid.

FIRST STEPS

Reformation of a disoriented institution such as education cannot happen overnight, nor can it be done in a haphazard manner. There must be a coherent strategy. What is needed are beachheads—a small number of adequately financed regional centers such as the College for Human Services in New York and the Oregon School of Community Services and Public Affairs to build new education with new professionals. Governors of states could be commissioned to generate total programs that would include the formulation of new curricula, the formation of a new organization with the consumer as an equal partner in governing that organization, and the preparation of community-based paraprofessionals to become credentialed teachers.

The issues before us are real. The crises are deep. The solutions require education. Paraprofessionals have achieved prominence in roles designed to patch up an unworkable system. They must become the central force in developing the education of the future—an education that prepares people for peace, social equality, and human organization.

It is a big challenge. It is a feasible challenge. Let us hope that we do not discover too late that for want of a paraprofessional, a civilization was lost.

NOTES

1. There was an equally optimistic, concurrent theme that projected a technical wonderland in which machines and other devices would produce enough goods and services to overcome all scarcities, and therefore persons would no longer have to work but could instead indulge in leisure and live on a guaranteed income. In the early stages this alternative did not militate against the paraprofessional movement because those who espoused it conceded that the poor could make use of their leisure time if they had access to a good education and training.

2. These maneuvers were cheap in the sense that the critics of education were unwilling to accept responsibility for any problems that children or youth have or for defining the consequences that would inevitably follow the elimination of schooling in a technological society.

3. The author's analysis in no way supports Daniel Bell's thinking that the 1960s were reactionary because the movements attempted to impede technological progress. The movements were reactionary, not because they impeded technological progress, but because they were incompetent.

4. Obviously, this argument contrasts sharply with that of Gartner and Riessman (1974), who attribute more power to consumers and more positive features to the various movements of the 1960s than does the author.

About the Authors

Alan Gartner is a professor at the Graduate School and University Center, City University of New York; co-director at the New Human Services Institute, Center for the Advanced Study of Education, City University of New York; and publisher of *Social Policy.* He is the author of *Paraprofessionals and Their Performance* (1971) and *The Preparation of Human Service Professionals* (1976).

Vivian Carter Jackson is a higher education associate at the Graduate School and University Center, City University of New York and director of the New Careers Training Laboratory.

Frank Riessman is a professor of education at Queens College; co-director of the New Human Services Institute, City University of New York; and the editor of *Social Policy.* He co-authored *New Careers for the Poor* (1965) and is the author of *The Inner City Child* (1976).

Don Davies is a professor of education and the director of the Institute for Responsive Education, Boston University. He was associate commissioner and subsequent deputy commissioner of the U.S. Office of Education.

Mary-Beth Fafard is associate professor of education at the University of Wisconsin at Milwaukee.

Musette El-Mohammed is associate coordinator of the Paraprofessional Teacher Education Program, Queens College.

Gina Schacter is a writer at the New Careers Training Laboratory, City University of New York, and editor of *City* a literary magazine.

Garda Bowman is a consultant in program analysis at the Bank Street College of Education, New York City.

Valerie C. Gilford is the director of the Cooperative

Education Program for Older Adults, New York City Community College, Division of Continuing Education.

Carla Drije is assistant director of the Office of Institutional Research and Program Evaluation, Brooklyn College.

Ursula Delworth is the director of the University Counselor Service and Professor of Counselor Education, University of Iowa.

Alan Sweet is the project administrator for the Minneapolis Public Schools/University of Minneapolis Teacher Center.

William F. Brown is professor of education and director of the Guidance Associate Programs, Southwest Texas State University, San Marcos.

Raymond Murphy is the executive assistant to the university dean for academic affairs, City University of New York.

William Thomas Carter is director, Division of Educational Systems Development, U.S. Office of Education.

Arthur Pearl is chair of the Committee on Education, University of California at Santa Cruz. He is the author of the *Atrocity of Education* (1973) and co-author of *New Careers for the Poor* (1965).